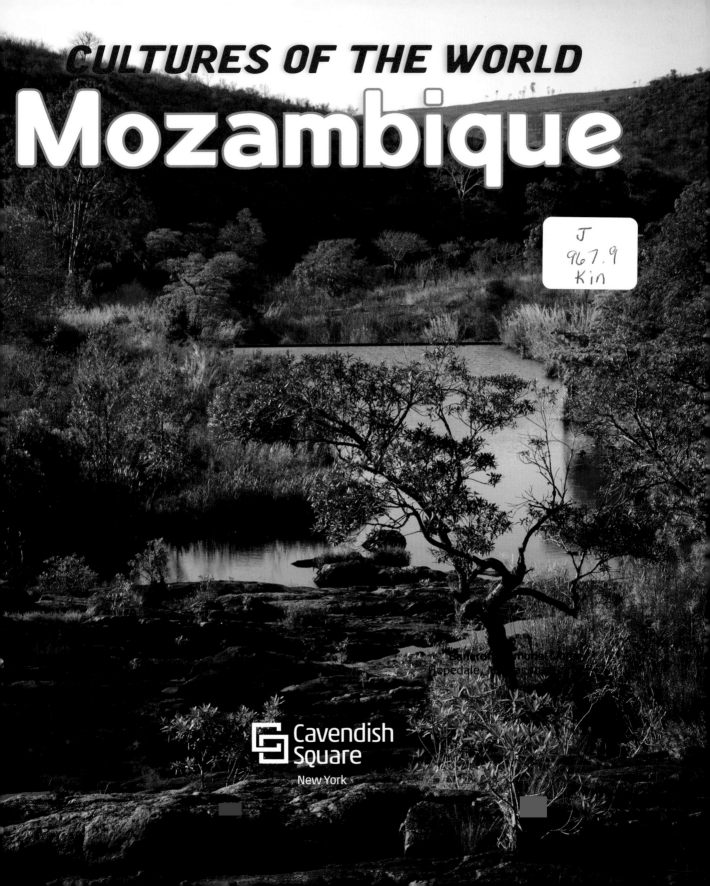

CULTURES OF THE WORLD
Mozambique

Cavendish
Square

New York

Published in 2021 by Cavendish Square Publishing, LLC
243 5th Avenue, Suite 136, New York, NY 10016
Copyright © 2021 by Cavendish Square Publishing, LLC

Third Edition

Website: cavendishsq.com

This publication represents the opinions and views of the author based on his or her personal experience, knowledge, and research. The information in this book serves as a general guide only. The author and publisher have used their best efforts in preparing this book and disclaim liability rising directly or indirectly from the use and application of this book.

All websites were available and accurate when this book was sent to press.

Library of Congress Cataloging-in-Publication Data

Names: King, David C., author. | Nevins, Debbie, author.
Title: Mozambique / David C. King and Debbie Nevins.
Other titles: Cultures of the world (third edition)
Description: Third edition. | New York : Cavendish Square Publishing, 2021.
 | Series: Cultures of the world | Includes bibliographical references
 and index.
Identifiers: LCCN 2020057781 | ISBN 9781502662590 (library binding) | ISBN
 9781502662606 (ebook)
Subjects: LCSH: Mozambique--Juvenile literature.
Classification: LCC DT3299 .K56 2021 | DDC 967.9--dc23
LC record available at https://lccn.loc.gov/2020057781

$29.⁶⁶

Writers, David C. King; Debbie Nevins, third edition
Editor, third edition: Debbie Nevins
Designer, third edition: Jessica Nevins
Picture Researcher, third edition: Jessica Nevins

Find us on

CONTENTS

MOZAMBIQUE TODAY

MOZAMBIQUE IS A WARM, VIBRANT COUNTRY ON THE COAST OF southeast Africa. It faces the Indian Ocean, with 1,535 miles (2,470 kilometers) of shoreline marked by sandy tropical beaches and port cities. Culturally, the country is a lively mix of African, Portuguese, Indian, and Brazilian influences, which show up in its music, dance, fashion, and cuisine.

With its wealth of natural resources—from a diversity of landscapes and wildlife to hidden deposits of minerals and natural gas—Mozambique should be thriving. This is not the case, however. Like many African nations, particularly those in the southern part of the continent, Mozambique is struggling mightily to climb out of extreme poverty brought on by centuries of colonial oppression.

The Portuguese first settled in Mozambique in the 16th century and eventually conquered the region, turning it into a colony—a situation that lasted well into the 20th century. When Mozambique finally gained its independence from Portugal in 1975, the future looked promising. It was already a popular destination for tourists drawn to the white-sand beaches and abundant wildlife. However, the country was soon torn apart by a vicious civil war. Then, in 2000, in the midst of rebuilding after peace was established, a flood devastated much of the country, destroying livestock and crops over a wide area. This scenario occurred yet again, and to an even greater extent, when back-to-back cyclones, Idai and Kenneth, hit the land in the spring of 2019. The massive destruction of lives and property greatly set back what economic progress had been achieved.

Mozambique is regularly affected by natural disasters—floods, cyclones, drought, and earthquakes. In fact, it's one of the most disaster-prone countries in the world, and this is only being made worse by climate change.

In 2020, another sort of disaster hit when the global COVID-19 pandemic swept across the country. Like much of Africa, Mozambique was hard hit by the earlier HIV/AIDS epidemic, which began in the 1980s. In 2016, it had the world's eighth-highest rate of HIV infection, with 12.3 percent of its adult population having the virus. The COVID-19 pandemic, therefore, compounded an existing public health emergency. The pandemic reached Mozambique in March 2020, at a vulnerable moment economically, as the country was still trying to recover from the devastating effects of cyclones Idai and Kenneth.

As of January 2021, Mozambique appeared to have dodged the worst of the COVID-19 bullet. There were 18,642 recorded cases, but only 166 deaths at that point. The government had imposed tough restrictions on gatherings, mask-wearing, and other measures, which apparently worked to keep the mortality rate to 0.8 percent, one of the lowest in the world. Indeed, the World Health Organization (WHO) praised the nation, saying Mozambique had the pandemic under control. Some other international observers, however, questioned the validity of the official statistics.

Either way, the full extent of the pandemic's effect on the economy will only eventually be revealed—but it certainly won't be good. The pandemic and its restrictions affected demand for goods and services across the globe. Reduced demand caused the prices of commodities to fall, which in turn slowed the pace of investment in gas and coal, two key industries for Mozambique.

If the Mozambican government demonstrated effective leadership in tackling the COVID-19 problem, then perhaps it will be successful in addressing the country's other problems—and there are many. Most problems stem from or reinforce extreme poverty, which provokes social dissatisfaction.

This is turn tends to trigger political unrest. In recent years, this instability is becoming more pronounced in a number of ways. In the northern province of Cabo Delgado, Islamist insurgents have been staging terrorist attacks since 2017. Media coverage of the hostilities there has been difficult to track as the government instituted a news blackout. Indeed, democracy has weakened as the government has

Outside a high school in Mozambique, students wear masks, practice social distancing, and wash their hands during the COVID-19 pandemic.

become more authoritarian. The organization Reporters Without Borders said in 2020 that "press freedom is in retreat in Mozambique" as journalists there continue to be harassed and intimidated.

Gender inequity, violence against women, malnutrition in children, inadequate education, unemployment, and substandard infrastructure are all among the very difficult problems facing Mozambique today. However, this doesn't mean there is no hope. Many spirited, determined, and hard-working people in this country are fighting to restore, elevate, and secure their beloved homeland. When seen through this lens, the future for Mozambique looks brighter.

GEOGRAPHY

Palm trees sway on a sandy beach in Pemba, Mozambique.

1

MOZAMBIQUE IS ONE OF 54 nations recognized by the United Nations (UN) on the continent of Africa. Located on the continent's southeastern coast, Mozambique faces the Indian Ocean. The country is narrow and elongated, edged by beautiful beaches set off by the lush green of palm trees and occasional mangrove swamps. Its coastline of 1,535 miles (2,470 km) is the third-longest on the continent.

On a map of Africa, Mozambique may appear to be relatively small, but that's deceptive because the continent itself is so enormous. In fact, while 15 other African nations are bigger, Mozambique is larger than the U.S. state of Texas. With a land area of 303,623 square miles (786,380 sq km), it is almost twice the size of California. Overlaid on a map of the eastern United States, Mozambique stretches from Canada to the Gulf of Mexico.

Mozambique borders Tanzania and Malawi to the north, Zambia and Zimbabwe to the west, and South Africa to the southwest. The tiny kingdom of Eswatini, also known as Swaziland, borders Mozambique to the southwest as well. Off the coast of Mozambique in the Indian Ocean is the African island nation of Madagascar.

REGIONS

The great Zambezi River forms a dividing line between northern and southern Mozambique. To the south of the river are the lowlands, less than 600 feet (183 meters) above sea level. This low-lying plain extends across almost the entire width of the country, except for highlands in the west called the Serra da Gorongosa, which include Mount Binga, the country's highest peak at 7,992 feet (2,436 m).

The southern plain is gently rolling land, with low hills and the wide deltas of several rivers. In the extreme south lies Delagoa Bay,

Farmers lead cattle through the fields of this agricultural nation.

a natural harbor on the east coast of Africa that is also known as Maputo Bay. Maputo, the capital of Mozambique, is situated on the bay.

The region north of the Zambezi differs from the south in several ways. Along the coast the sandy stretches are broken up by rocky cliffs and headlands. There are many offshore islands, some of which are coral formations. In addition to the Zambezi, more than 30 rivers flow eastward to the ocean, while the Rovuma River in the far north forms Mozambique's border with Tanzania.

Except for the Serra da Gorongosa, all of Mozambique's higher, more rugged lands lie north of the Zambezi. The coastal plain gives way to a higher plateau, and, toward the western borders, the land rises to mountainous terrain, with several peaks above 7,000 feet (2,134 m).

Mozambique is divided into 10 provinces and one capital city (Maputo) with provincial status. Zambezia and Nampula provinces, in the north, have the best farmland and are home to about 40 percent of the people. By contrast, Maputo and Gaza provinces in the south are thinly populated as you get closer to the interiors of the provinces.

Although Mozambique is primarily an agricultural nation, with only around 37 percent of the population living in urban areas, there are a number of cities. Only Maputo, formerly known as Lourenço Marques, has a population over 1 million (1,088,449, as of the 2017 census; or 2,717,437 including the

surrounding metropolitan area). Other major cities include Nampula, called "the capital of the north," with a population of 743,125; the coastal city of Beira, with a population of 533,825; Chimoio (372,821 residents); and the seaport of Quelimane (349,842 residents).

Mozambique's capital city, Maputo, gleams in the sunshine.

RIVERS AND LAKES

Mozambique has 104 rivers that drain to the Indian Ocean. Many are tributaries of larger rivers that rise in the western highlands. The Zambezi River, which dominates central Mozambique, is one of the world's largest rivers and the fourth largest in Africa. It is the longest African river that flows to the Indian Ocean. As it nears the coast, the river becomes as wide as 2 miles (3 km) across.

This aerial view of a river delta in Mozambique shows how rivers flow together as they reach the ocean.

Both the Rovuma and Lugenda rivers are important sources of water to the north, providing water for irrigation. South of the Zambezi, the major rivers are the Pungwe, Save (Sabi), Limpopo, and Komati. The Limpopo River is the 10th largest in Africa. Many of Mozambique's older towns were built at the mouths of rivers, as they provided trade routes to the interior. The rivers are useful for canoe travel, but larger modern vessels can only navigate the deeper waters of the Zambezi. Many of the rivers have wide fluctuations in their volume of water between the wet and dry seasons, and the shallow channels often shift course.

Lake Niassa is partly in Malawi and Tanzania, but about one-third of it, or 5,000 square miles (13,000 sq km), lies within Mozambique. This dramatically beautiful lake is the third largest and second deepest in Africa. It lies at the southern end of the Great Rift Valley (part of the East African Rift System), the mammoth geological trench that stretches from the Red Sea south through Africa into Mozambique. The lake, also known as Lake Malawi in Malawi and Lake Nyasa in Tanzania, is surrounded by the steep slopes of the rift valley. The crystal clear waters contain a greater number of indigenous, or native, fish species than any other lake in the world. Lake Niassa is also famous for its spectacular sunsets.

Another major lake was formed by the building of the Cahora Bassa Dam. The dam, which was built on the Zambezi River between 1969 and 1974, is the fifth largest in the world, and the lake it created, the Cahora Bassa, covers an area of 1,000 square miles (2,590 sq km).

CLIMATE

Mozambique has a tropical maritime climate, which normally would mean high levels of precipitation. Because of the prevailing winds, however, the moisture

RAMSAR SITES

The Ramsar Convention on Wetlands is an international treaty for the conservation and sustainable use of wetlands. The treaty dates to 1971 and is named for the Iranian city of Ramsar where it was signed. The convention uses a broad definition of wetlands— it includes all lakes and rivers, underground aquifers, swamps and marshes, wet grasslands, peatlands, oases, estuaries, deltas and tidal flats, mangroves and other coastal areas, coral reefs, and all human-made sites such as fish ponds, rice paddies, reservoirs, and salt pans.

Wetlands are of vital importance, according to the convention, because they are among the world's most productive environments. They are ecosystems of "biological diversity that provide the water and productivity upon which countless species of plants and animals depend for survival."

As part of its mission, the convention identifies wetlands sites around the world that are of international importance and works to protect them. Of the 2,410 Ramsar sites (as of 2020), Mozambique has two, with a combined surface area of 11,205,913 acres (4,534,872 hectares). They are Lake Niassa (shown here) and its Coastal Zone, and the Zambezi Delta, where the river meets the ocean.

According to the Ramsar listing, Lake Niassa supports "threatened populations of leopard, sable antelope, and elephants...The lake also lies within flyways of migratory birds that use the lake margins as staging areas between Africa and Europe."

The Zambezi Delta is "one of the most diverse and productive river delta systems in the world...home to a significant population of large mammals including the African buffalo, elephant, hippopotamus, lion and leopard. [Its] large concentration of waterbird species [includes] white-backed and pink-backed pelicans, herons, flamingos, egrets, African fish eagles, storks, Caspian terns, wattled cranes, and endangered grey crowned cranes."

Fields were flooded following Cyclone Idai in March 2019.

generally bypasses Mozambique and rainfall amounts are spotty—high in some areas, very low in others. Maputo, for example, averages only 30 inches (760 millimeters) of rainfall a year, while the northwest highlands receive as much as 80 inches (2,000 mm) per year. The lack of rainfall sometimes creates severe drought conditions in the south, destroying crops and livestock. Too much rain, however, has also led to devastation by causing rivers to overflow, as occurred during particularly disastrous floods in early 2000 and early 2001. In 2000, five weeks of heavy rainfall in February and March caused flooding that left around 800 people dead. It was the country's worst flood in 50 years.

In addition to regional variations, rainfall amounts and temperatures fluctuate with the two main seasons: a wet season from November to March and a longer dry period from April to October. In the southern lowlands, January temperatures range from 79 degrees to 86 degrees Fahrenheit (26 degrees to 30 degrees Celsius), and in the more comfortable dry season, the range is about 20 degrees cooler. The highlands of the north are cooler throughout the year, with January averages of 71°F to 77°F (22°C to 25°C) and July ranges from 52°F to 59°F (11°C to 15°C).

VEGETATION

Most of Mozambique's vegetation is savanna (grasslands) and tropical forest. Along the coast, coconut palms are common, with some others, including date palms, also plentiful. Along the well-drained slopes of the hills, there are scattered patches of forest, including stands of ebony and ironwood. Along the upper reaches of the rivers, especially the Zambezi and the Limpopo, the mopani tree, a form of ironwood valued for long-lasting lumber, is common. The most distinct tree of the savanna is the baobab. Stretches of mangrove

THE BAOBAB TREE

One of the most striking trees in Mozambique is the baobab. This iconic tree is often called Africa's "Tree of Life," and it grows in 32 African countries. It has a fat, barrel-shaped trunk that can reach 30 feet (9 m) in diameter and short, thin branches, giving rise to the legend that the gods planted it upside down, with its roots thrust in the air. Adding to its legendary status is the fact that a tree can live for more than 2,000 years. (Some claims say 5,000 or even 6,000 years!)

The baobab has large, gourd-like fruit with a sweet, tasty pulp. People use the strong fiber from the bark to make rope and even cloth, and they sometimes hollow out the trunk for storing water or to use as a temporary shelter. The leaves, when carefully treated, are cooked as vegetables.

are found along the coast, while bamboo and spear grass are abundant along the river banks.

WILDLIFE

Hunting, poaching, severe drought, and a long civil war (1977–1992) have combined to decimate the country's wildlife in some areas, but Mozambique still has a rich and varied fauna. Savanna areas are home to such well-known species as the elephant, rhinoceros, and giraffe, as well as packs of spotted hyena, jackal, and wild dog. Herd animals such as antelope, African buffalo, and zebra are common, as are the predators that stalk them, including cheetahs and lions. Hippopotamuses are common in the lower reaches of the rivers, along with crocodiles. Other abundant species are warthogs, monkeys, and baboons, plus a variety of snakes, including the cobra, python, puff adder, and viper.

The years of civil war directly affected some areas that were the focus of fighting, including Gorongosa National Park and the land around it. The

A warthog grazes in Gorongosa National Park.

civil war was also destructive because at that time there was no control over poachers. The elephant population, for example, which once numbered more than 54,000, had dwindled to about 10,800 in 2019.

As in other countries, human population growth and urbanization are shrinking the habitat available to wildlife. This is affecting Mozambique's bird population as well. Experts estimate that 690 bird species are either residents or regular migrating visitors to Mozambique, including its offshore islands. Many of the birds have colorful names, such as yellow-breasted hylotia, cardinal quela, East African swee, white-tailed blue fly catcher, and Zanzibar red bishop. Species in the country's northeast include large birds such as flamingos, cranes, herons, storks, pelicans, and ibis. Deeper inland, quail, guinea fowl, partridge, wild geese, and wild ducks are abundant.

Off the coast of the province of Inhambane in the south, the six islands of the Bazaruto Archipelago feature a wonderful assortment of wildlife. The clear coastal waters are filled with brightly colored fish. Farther out to sea are the migratory routes of humpback whales and bottlenose and humpback dolphins; there are also game fish, such as marlins and sailfish. The islands are home to Mozambique's last remaining population of dugong, a marine mammal related to the manatee.

The Bazaruto Archipelago support an abundance of wildlife habitats: more than 170 bird species, 48 reptile species, 21 species of terrestrial mammals, 9 species of marine mammals, 500 species of marine and coastal mollusks, and 2,000 fish species. The islands are also home to around 5,000 people.

INTERNET LINKS

www.fao.org/3/i9805en/I9805EN.pdf
The UN's Food and Agriculture Organization country profile for Mozambique includes information about geography, climate, and population.

www.worldatlas.com/maps/mozambique
This site offers maps and geographical information.

HISTORY

A cannon stands ready to protect against invaders in the old Portuguese fort in Maputo. Built in 1781, the fort is now a tourist attraction.

2

THE HISTORY OF MOZAMBIQUE dates far back into the mists of time—long, long before Europeans first set foot on the land. Nevertheless, their arrival about five centuries ago began a new chapter in the region's long story.

In the year 1498, a fleet of four Portuguese ships commanded by the explorer Vasco da Gama sailed around the Cape of Good Hope, the southern tip of Africa. From there, the fleet sailed northeasterly up the coast into waters previously unknown to European sailors and landed on the Island of Mozambique (off the coast of today's city of Nampula). Da Gama stopped there briefly, and although the island was already populated by people who had lived there for centuries, he claimed it for Portugal. Da Gama then sailed on to India. His historic voyage opened a trade route between Europe and India, China, and what were called the Spice Islands (modern Indonesia).

At the same time, the Italian explorer Christopher Columbus was probing the coasts of the Americas for Spain, hoping to find a westward route to those same fabled kingdoms of Asia, with their treasures of silk, ivory, jade, tea, and spices. These expeditions would gradually bring all the world's regions into a global economic network. Mozambique was soon to play an important part in that emerging international trade. Gold, ivory, and later, enslaved peoples were transported from Africa's interior to the coast and then shipped to distant ports in Europe, Asia, and the Americas.

When Vasco da Gama "discovered" Mozambique Island, the region that would become Mozambique had already had a long and colorful history.

Rock art images of hunter-gatherers at the Chinamapere archaeological landscape in Manica date back thousands of years. Some Mozambicans consider the site to be a sacred place for communication with ancestors.

EARLY HISTORY

The earliest evidence of human life has been found in the Rift Valley in East Africa, which runs from the Red Sea south to Mozambique. Although there is little fossil evidence in Mozambique, it is safe to say that humans and human-like creatures have lived in this region for a million years or more.

Little is known of the early inhabitants—small groups that lived by hunting and gathering food in the wild. By 100 CE, perhaps earlier, Bantu-speaking groups began moving into the area. The Bantu sustained themselves by farming and raising cattle. They slowly spread eastward from the highlands, reaching the coast of the Indian Ocean by about 400 CE.

The Bantu settlements became increasingly complex. Some people became skilled workers and built stone enclosures around their settlements. Several powerful chiefdoms emerged, including the Makua, north of the Zambezi River, and the Karanga in the south.

COASTAL TRADE

Around 900 CE, Arab traders began establishing trading posts along the coast of present-day Mozambique. There had long been a prosperous trade along the east coast of Africa, but until 900 CE, it had not reached so far south. The ancient Egyptians had traded along that northern part of the east coast as early as 2500 BCE. They were later followed by the Phoenicians, Greeks, and Romans. After the fall of the Roman Empire in the fifth century CE, there was a decline in the coastal trade until Arab Muslims (followers of the religion of Islam) revived it.

The Muslim posts on the coast connected Mozambique to the existing trade routes with the Mediterranean world and also with ports in India and Asia. A town called Sofala, near the mouth of the Buzi River in what is now central Mozambique, became the major trading port. Gold, ivory, iron goods, copper, and cotton were taken from the interior, with the gold from what is now modern-day Zimbabwe being the most important commodity. Sofala, which no longer exists today, became a prosperous town of about 10,000 people.

Other Muslim commercial settlements also developed north of Sofala. Most of the coastal towns were controlled by Arab sultans, and many of the people had converted to Islam. Caravans carrying cloth, beads, and other goods wound their way up the Zambezi and other rivers into Zimbabwe, returning to the coast with gold and other goods.

A struggle developed for control of this profitable trade. Gradually, the cattle-raising Karanga people won out in the south, while the Makua people took control of the north. By about 1100, the trade began to involve enslaved people from the interior.

THE ARRIVAL OF THE PORTUGUESE

As soon as the king of Portugal learned of the gold trade in Mozambique, he sent expeditions to find out more. By 1502, the Portuguese had made a settlement at

Sofala, a gold exporting center, and in 1507, they occupied Mozambique Island to serve as a way station on trading voyages to India and the Spice Islands. By 1530, they controlled much of the coast, forcing the Muslim traders to relocate.

The Portuguese were eager to reach the source of the gold in Zimbabwe, but they continually encountered stiff resistance from its inhabitants. In 1561, the Shona people killed Gonçalo da Silveira, a Jesuit priest and the head of the first mission in eastern Africa. In response, Portugal sent a large army, which spent the years from 1569 to 1575 trying to conquer the central African gold-mining region. Most of the soldiers died of diseases carried by either mosquitoes or tsetse flies. Of one force of 1,000 men sent out in 1572, for example, only 180 returned.

By the end of the 16th century, consequently, most of Mozambique remained beyond Portuguese control. The Portuguese occupied the lower Zambezi Valley and established bases at Sena and Tete on the Zambezi River. However, the rest of the area remained fragmented.

The 16th-century Fort São Sebastião sits on the northern tip of the Island of Mozambique.

SMALL HOLDINGS

Eventually, other European countries became interested in grabbing parts of Africa. In 1607 and 1608, the Dutch made two attempts to take Mozambique Island. Both attacks failed, but they made the Portuguese aware of how insecure and vulnerable their hold on the region was. Consequently, they again tried to conquer the interior, and for a time, they controlled a large area from the coast inland to the northern part of present-day Zimbabwe. They also managed to extend their coastal holdings and, in 1781, permanently occupied Delagoa Bay (at the site of modern Maputo), driving out Dutch and Austrian traders.

Until the late 1800s, Mozambique was not a Portuguese colony in the usual sense of the word. Through most of the 17th and 18th centuries, the region was a patchwork of small holdings. Some of these holdings were ruled by men who had deserted formal Portuguese settlements. They intermarried with local women, creating a mixed-race group known as *mestiços*. Some mestiços, as well as a number of Portuguese settlers, were granted estates by the king of Portugal. These estates, called *prazos*, were given to settlers and wealthy traders and were located mostly in the Zambezi Valley. The rulers of the estates, called *prazeros*, governed with absolute authority, much like the monarchs of feudal kingdoms in Europe during the Middle Ages. They kept control by granting more prazos to Europeans. (Although modified over time, the prazo system of land use continued until the 1930s.)

Even though the Portuguese managed to set up armed mining camps, their hold over the interior slowly weakened. In 1693, a chief of the Changamire people led an uprising that forced the Portuguese out of the highlands.

MOZAMBIQUE AND THE SLAVE TRADE

The gold trade declined in the 18th century, but it was replaced by trade with the interior for ivory and enslaved peoples. The slave trade had existed on a small scale even before the arrival of the Europeans. The growth of European-controlled plantations in both the West Indies and East Indies led to a steadily increasing demand for enslaved peoples and perpetuated the slave trade, a practice that involved both Africans and Europeans.

DAVID LIVINGSTONE

A Scottish missionary and explorer named David Livingstone made three extraordinary journeys to the interior of Africa, launching his daring ventures from the mouth of the Zambezi River in Mozambique. In the mid-1850s, he made his way up the Zambezi and crossed the continent to Luanda (in present-day Angola) on the Atlantic Coast. To get his party of Mozambicans back to their homes, he retraced his route across Africa. His last expedition included a search for the source of the Nile River.

David Livingstone is shown here in a photograph taken around the 1850s.

After years of being out of contact with the outside world, Livingstone was found in 1871, sick and starving, by the American journalist Henry M. Stanley. In 1869, Stanley had been sent by his newspaper, the New York Herald, *to explore rumors that Livingstone was dead. After exploring together for a while, Stanley returned to Western society. Livingstone continued his work for another year and died at his camp in Zambia, still exploring and writing.*

Livingstone's 30 years of exploration and missionary work had a powerful effect on the West's knowledge of Africa and attitudes toward its people. He also campaigned vigorously for an end to the slave trade.

Changes in climate affected the slave trade. Mozambique suffered a series of disastrous droughts between about 1790 and the early 1830s; as crops failed and cattle wealth declined, a growing number of people turned to banditry and slave raiding. More and more caravans arrived at the coast with their cargos of chained, frightened villagers from the interior. By 1800, Mozambique was one of the world's major centers of slave trading. Between 1825 and 1830, enslaved peoples were shipped from Mozambican ports at the rate of 25,000 per year. While many were sold to plantations in the East Indies, thousands also ended up in Brazil, the West Indies, and the United States.

In 1836, under pressure from Great Britain, the government of Portugal outlawed the slave trade, a move that inadvertently served to drive the cruel activities underground. It is estimated that at least 1 million Africans were shipped from Mozambican ports during the 19th century.

THE 19TH CENTURY

The series of droughts that ravaged Mozambique in the late 18th and early 19th centuries provided opportunities for strong African chiefs to gain control over larger areas. The Nguni people became highly militaristic, and three powerful kingdoms emerged: the Zulu, the Swazi, and the Ndandwe. These kingdoms, and other groups in the border region between Mozambique and Zimbabwe, engaged in a series of raids and minor wars through the first half of the 19th century.

The droughts also destroyed much of the agricultural economy of the Zambezi Valley, driving many prazeros to abandon their estates. By the 1850s, the region was divided into five large feudal estates ruled primarily by mestiço families. Like the feuding kingdoms of the highlands, the valley families bickered and fought with each other and with the Portuguese colonial government.

Throughout much of the century, Portugal also struggled to prevent Mozambique from falling into British hands. In the early 1800s, the British took control of Cape Colony and then tried to seize the southern portion of Delagoa Bay. Portugal objected and so did the Boer Republic (now the Republic of South Africa). In 1875, France served as arbitrator in the dispute and gave the entire bay to Portuguese Mozambique. After a few more years of arguing, Britain and Portugal signed a treaty in May 1891, giving Mozambique its modern geopolitical shape, although the British gained large areas of the highlands, which are now part of Zimbabwe.

Another 19th-century development was Portugal's invitation to European companies to start plantations to cultivate sugarcane and cotton and grow sunflower seeds (for oil). These concessions stimulated the Mozambican economy, providing money for improvements in vital infrastructure such as

The nations of Africa are a relatively modern creation. As recently as the 19th century, vast regions of the continent's interior remained unmapped and unknown to the outside world. Native peoples lived in various tribal kingdoms with their own rich cultures and traditions. To Europe and the rest of the Western world, though, Africa was "the dark continent." In this case, "dark" meant not only unexplored but also wild.

Africa's seacoast regions were more accessible and therefore better known to Europeans. Beginning in the 15th century, Portugal and other nations set up trading posts and forts and attempted colonies along coastal areas. North Africa, however, had long been dominated by Muslim cultures and was essentially a barrier to Europe. Until the 18th and 19th centuries, European powers were more interested in the Americas.

European colonies in the Americas eventually won their independence. At the same time, the Industrial Revolution was radically changing Western economies and ways of life. For these and other reasons, Europeans took another look at Africa. They sent explorers into the heart of Africa to map it, convinced that the African people needed the "civilizing" influence of European culture, even though the African people had their own unique cultures.

Europe, therefore, began to see Africa as ripe for the taking, and a virtual land grab began. By 1884 and 1885, what has come to be called "the Scramble for Africa" was on. A new age of imperialism began in which major Western powers tried to secure and gain supremacy by building an empire of overseas properties. Colonies were a status symbol as well as a source of native resources, labor, and military recruits.

In 1884, a group of 13 European countries met in Berlin, Germany, to draw up the rules of African colonization and literally split the continent among themselves. The colonizing powers were primarily Britain and France, with Germany, Italy, Portugal, Belgium, and Spain taking the rest. The Portuguese had hoped that they would gain large areas, especially along the coast, on the basis of their many voyages of discovery. However, the European colonial powers granted most large areas to Great Britain. However, Portugal did retain control of Mozambique, along with Angola and a few other smaller holdings.

Lines of new nations were drawn arbitrarily, sometimes cutting apart historically tribal regions. By 1902, 90 percent of Africa was under European control. By 1914, the European takeover of Africa was complete, with only Ethiopia managing to remain sovereign.

roads and ports. The growing number of European companies also helped to counter British influence in the area.

THE COLONIAL PERIOD

Beginning in 1895 with the conquest of the Gaza Empire, Portugal exercised increasing control over Mozambique. Large areas of the country, however, were administered by two large private corporations—the Mozambique Company and the Niassa Company. The companies often forced indigenous workers to labor under brutal conditions, and more than 10,000 people were sent each year to work in the gold mines of South Africa.

During the early years of the 20th century, Portugal made sporadic attempts to create unified control over the colony. The city of Lourenço Marques (modern Maputo) was established as the capital of Mozambique, replacing Mozambique Island. In 1917, an uprising by the Makonde people in Zambezia Province was crushed after bitter fighting. This marked the end of resistance to Portuguese rule.

Private companies continued to dominate Mozambique until 1926, when a revolution in Portugal led to the rise of a Fascist dictator, Antonio de Oliveira Salazar. Salazar ruled Portugal with an iron fist as prime minister from 1932 to 1968. He brought company rule to an end and established direct and centralized control over all of Mozambique.

Salazar established a "planned economy," in which Portugal would be the source of manufactured goods and Portugal's colonies would produce food and raw materials. Company powers were eliminated, and the system of prazos was ended. Forced labor was replaced by forced agricultural systems, in which farmers were told precisely what crops to grow. This led to a tremendous increase in the production of rice and cotton between 1930 and 1950.

Portugal remained neutral during World War II (1939—1945) and enjoyed considerable prosperity through the export of food and raw materials. After the war, Salazar softened his Fascist policies. Some industries were developed, and Mozambique's beaches and wildlife began to draw tourists, especially from South Africa.

The increase in Mozambique's exports did not produce a significant change in the standard of living of the people, however. In the planned economy, little attention was paid to crops needed for subsistence, and the practice of shipping workers to the South African mines continued. Salazar also encouraged white settlers to move into southern Mozambique, and, partly as a result, the number of white settlers increased to roughly 200,000.

THE MOVEMENT FOR INDEPENDENCE

In the years following World War II, Europe's colonies in Africa were rocked with demands for independence. Many of the movements were started by veterans who had served in the Allied military forces during World War II, when they fought to free people from the tyranny and atrocities of Nazi Germany. Throughout the 1960s and 1970s, country after country won its independence.

The movement for independence began late in Mozambique, probably because Portugal had remained neutral in the war, so there were no veterans of the Portuguese military returning to Mozambique. In 1962, a group of exiled Mozambicans met in Tanzania, where they formed an organization called the Front for the Liberation of Mozambique (FRELIMO). Its leader was Eduardo C. Mondlane, a Mozambican scholar who had been living in the United States.

Once Portugal refused to negotiate independence, FRELIMO decided on guerrilla warfare. By late 1965, FRELIMO troops had gained control of large areas in the north. The Portuguese government retaliated, arresting 1,500 FRELIMO agents and driving the movement out of the south. At the same time, the government launched a major development program. Jobs were created by the start of the construction on the mammoth Cahora Bassa Dam. The building of roads, schools, and hospitals also stimulated economic growth and, it was hoped, increased loyalty to Portugal.

In spite of Portugal's efforts, FRELIMO continued its activities, at least in the north. In 1969, a letter bomb killed Mondlane, and the movement's military commander, Samora Machel, took over as party president in May 1970.

Machel continued the war for liberation. When Portugal sent an additional 35,000 troops, FRELIMO returned to guerrilla warfare, including the disruption of work on the Cahora Bassa Dam. How much these activities contributed

to Mozambique's eventual independence is uncertain because the matter was finally decided by events in Portugal. Salazar's health failed in 1968, and a struggle for control followed into the early 1970s. A left-wing military revolution in 1974 produced a new Portuguese government that had no interest in maintaining colonies. FRELIMO, headed by Machel, became increasingly influential in Mozambique. In September 1974, Mozambique was granted its independence. A transitional government, with Machel as president, was installed, and Mozambique became officially independent on June 25, 1975.

The decaying Vila Algarve was once the headquarters of the Portuguese Secret Police (PIDE), renowned for its brutality and use of torture during Mozambique's struggle for independence.

CIVIL WAR

The FRELIMO organization assumed power in a one-party government that had no experience in self-government. Samora Machel was president from 1975 until his death in a suspicious plane crash in 1986. Today, Machel is regarded as a hero, the founder of modern Mozambique who freed the nation from oppression.

Machel had tried to establish a Marxist government with dictatorial powers similar to the governments of the former Soviet Union and other Communist states. However, he and FRELIMO had little chance for success for several reasons. Many educated people and skilled workers had left the country rather than stay in a Marxist society. In addition, the world economy was in chaos following the oil crisis of 1973. Perhaps the most serious obstacle to success was FRELIMO's support of liberation movements by black people in Southern Rhodesia (now Zimbabwe) and South Africa. In retaliation, the white governments of Rhodesia and South Africa, along with anti-Communist groups in the United States and Europe, tried to undermine FRELIMO's control. They formed a militant force of their own called the Mozambican National Resistance, or RENAMO. In 1977, RENAMO launched a bloody civil war that devastated Mozambique for more than 15 years.

President Samora Machel speaks to a crowd in Maputo on the first anniversary of the nation's independence: June 25, 1976.

In spite of increasing opposition and violence, the FRELIMO government had some success, particularly in social matters. A major education program was started to overcome the country's literacy rate of less than 5 percent. Attendance doubled in primary schools and increased sevenfold in secondary schools. Although there were only 100 trained doctors in the entire country, a massive immunization program reached 90 percent of the population within 5 years. Another significant change was in promoting the rights of women. In the 1977 elections for popular assemblies, 28 percent of the seats were won by women, one of the highest rates in the world.

However, the FRELIMO government could not overcome the powerful RENAMO force. In 1980, RENAMO began destroying schools, factories, railroads, and government installations. Within a few years, the government had undisputed control only over a few cities, and travel became increasingly dangerous. Bands of guerrillas roamed the countryside, raiding villages to meet their daily needs.

With tens of thousands of his country's citizens killed and the economy in ruins, President Machel met with the presidents of Zimbabwe and Zambia in 1986, hoping to end some of the outside support for RENAMO. On the return flight to Maputo, it was reported that Machel's plane was diverted by a South African radio signal and crashed in South African territory under very suspicious circumstances, killing the president. He was succeeded by Joaquim Chissano, who was elected by FRELIMO as Mozambique's new president.

In 1990, FRELIMO adopted a new constitution, ending the party's Marxist policies and allowing multiparty elections. The civil war dragged on until 1992, however, when a meeting known as the Rome Conference led to a cease-fire and a peace agreement being signed between President Chissano and the RENAMO leader, Afonso Dhlakama. The killing and destruction had finally ended, but Mozambique lay in ruins. The future did not look very bright.

DEMOCRACY

Mozambique's first democratic elections were held in October 1994. Chissano won 53 percent of the vote, and Dhlakama won 34 percent. The two parties divided the seats in the parliament, called the Assembly of the Republic, or

National Assembly. A United Nations (UN) force, ONUMOZ, entered the country to ensure the peace and to oversee the elections. ONUMOZ completed its work and left the country in early 1995.

Chissano's government faced the Herculean task of rebuilding the economy while reintegrating 1.7 million refugees into the country along with thousands of former soldiers from both sides in the long civil war. With considerable foreign aid, the government made slow but steady progress in national reconstruction.

CHALLENGES OF THE 21ST CENTURY

Economic reconstruction received a severe blow in February 2000 when Mozambique experienced one of the worst floods in its modern history. After a month of heavy rain and a cyclone, the rivers in southern and central regions overflowed their banks. Seven hundred people died in the floods, and roughly half a million were left homeless. The partially restored roads, bridges, and railway lines were again destroyed, and about 80 percent of the livestock died. The flood also dislodged hundreds of land mines laid during the war and randomly deposited them elsewhere.

Mozambique again began rebuilding itself. Chissano, who had been re-elected in 1999, stepped down as president in 2004. FRELIMO's candidate, Armando Guebuza, defeated RENAMO's Afonso Dhlakama and became the next president.

However, Dhlakama was not about to give up. In 2011, he announced that RENAMO was preparing a revolution against the existing government. Over the next several years, RENAMO militants staged various low-level attacks against police, military, and government forces. Fighting took place mainly in the northwestern part of the country, and thousands of local people there fled to neighboring Malawi to escape the violence.

Against this background, the 2014 elections were hotly contested, but FRELIMO's candidate, Filipe Nyusi, managed a win. He and Dhlakama pursued peace talks for the next several years until Dhlakama's sudden death in 2018 of a heart attack. After losing its leader, RENAMO regrouped under Ossufo Momade, and peace negotiations continued.

In March 2019, Cyclone Idai devastated a large portion of Mozambique, killing around 600 people. The following month, another cyclone killed more than 40 people in the north. The two weather events left more than 162,000 Mozambicans homeless, further adding to the country's difficulties.

A LASTING PEACE?

On August 1, 2019, Momade agreed to renounce violence and signed a peace agreement with President Nyusi at RENAMO's remote military base in the Gorongosa Mountains. With that, the last remaining members of the insurgency surrendered their weapons. At a second signing ceremony in Mapotu's Peace Square, Momade said, "We will no longer commit the mistakes of the past." He stated that he and RENAMO would now focus on "maintaining peace and national reconciliation."

Filipe Nyusi went on to win a second term as president that year despite isolated reports of election-related violence, voter intimidation, and fraud. Nyusi was sworn in on January 15, 2020, a year that would bring a whole new set of problems to Mozambique.

INTERNET LINKS

www.nationalgeographic.com/travel/destinations/africa/mozambique/island-of-mozambique-unesco-world-heritage-site
This photo essay explores the historic island of Mozambique.

www.pbs.org/empires/victoria/empire/livingstone.html
A quick biography of David Livingstone is provided on this site.

www.thoughtco.com/what-caused-the-scramble-for-africa-43730
This article is an overview, with links, of the events that led to the rapid colonization of Africa by Europe in the late 19th century.

GOVERNMENT

A huge statue of Samora Machel stands outside City Hall in Maputo. Donated in 2011 by North Korea, the statue has been criticized for bearing little resemblance to Machel.

3

R ARELY DO FORMER COLONIES transition to independence easily. For the emerging nation, the process is an act of reinvention after decades, or even centuries, of submission and oppression by an outside force. The departure of that colonizing authority leaves the vulnerable new nation with a power vacuum. Many newly independent countries explode into civil war or quickly find themselves under the thumb of a dictator. This new oppressor is often seen at first as a hero in the heady but unsettled new days of independence, but sometimes the hero takes advantage of the young nation's fragility and builds a government based on his own absolute authority.

So it was in Mozambique. During its first 30 years of independence, the country faced extraordinary obstacles. The leaders of the FRELIMO independence movement who formed the first government in 1975 had no previous experience in political matters. When the Portuguese granted

Mozambique independence, they had allowed for only a nine-month transition period to self-rule—hardly enough time to prepare to run a country.

FRELIMO formed a one-party state committed to building a Marxist-Leninist, or Communist, society similar to the former Soviet Union. This determination led many business owners and others to leave the country rather than live in a Communist society.

The most serious obstacle to the establishment of a stable and successful government in Mozambique was the opposition of anti-Communist groups based outside Mozambique. These resistance groups formed the National Resistance Movement, or RENAMO. They received funds and military training from the white-controlled governments of Rhodesia (now Zimbabwe) and South Africa. In 1977, RENAMO's guerrilla tactics plunged the country into the disastrous civil war that plagued Mozambique until 1992.

THE SEARCH FOR STABILITY

The first important steps to a more democratic government were taken in 1990 when FRELIMO unveiled a new constitution that abandoned the party's experiment in Communism and provided for multiparty elections. In

A woman casts her ballot at a polling station in Maputo during the October 2018 elections.

the elections of 1994 and 1999, President Joaquim Chissano defeated the RENAMO leader Alfonso Dhlakama in a close vote, winning with only a 4 percent margin in 1999. FRELIMO also kept its majority in parliament, the 250-member National Assembly, with 133 of the seats in 1998. RENAMO claimed that the counting of the votes had been fraudulent. Foreign observers and the Mozambique Supreme Court, however, declared that the elections had been legitimate.

The Chissano government continued to face great difficulties. The enormous damage from the civil war would require years to repair. Moreover, Mozambique faced one of the largest repatriations in African history as 1.7 million refugees returned from having sought asylum in the neighboring countries of Malawi, Zimbabwe, Swaziland, Zambia, Tanzania, and South Africa. Another 4 million Mozambicans who had been internally displaced by warfare or drought returned to their homes in the late 1990s. The disastrous flooding in 2000 and 2001 compounded all the existing problems.

The year 2004 was important for Mozambique. In the December elections, President Chissano decided to step down, and his party's handpicked successor, Armando Guebuza, was elected president. FRELIMO also won easily in the parliamentary elections, gaining nearly two-thirds of the seats in the National Assembly. Luisa Diogo was appointed prime minister, the first Mozambican woman to attain such a high office, which she held until 2010.

To date, the FRELIMO party has managed to hold on to majority power as the country struggles with democracy. In 2015, Filipe Nyusi became president and was re-elected in 2019 following elections marred by violence, voter intimidation, and fraud.

President Filipe Nyusi addresses the nation during his inauguration ceremony on January 15, 2015.

THE BRANCHES OF GOVERNMENT

Mozambique is a presidential republic. The executive branch of the government is headed by the president, who is both the head of state and the commander in chief. The president is responsible for seeing that legislation is enforced,

DEMOCRACY IN MOZAMBIQUE?

International observers find Mozambique to be only partially successful, if at all, in its quest to become a democratic nation. In general, as of early 2021, the country seems to be on a dangerous downward trajectory in this respect.

Freedom House is a U.S.-based independent watchdog organization that conducts research and advocacy on democracy, political freedom, and human rights. In its 2020 "Freedom in the World" report, it ranked Mozambique as "Partly Free," with a score of 45 out of 100—down from a score of 51 in 2019—in which 100 represents a fully free society. (That year, Norway, Sweden, and Finland scored 100, with South Sudan coming in last with a "Not Free" score of -2.) The report cites violence against opposition politicians and intimidation of poll workers and journalists, including alleged state complicity in the murder of Anastácio Matavel, a respected independent election observer. The report also states corruption as a major obstacle to democracy in Mozambique.

Another organization, the Economist Intelligence Unit (EIU), a London-based research and analysis company, ranked Mozambique at 120 out of 167 nations in its 2019 Democracy Index. (Number 1 represents the best example of a full democracy— that year it was Norway—and number 167—that year, North Korea—the worst.) The Democracy Index classifies each country as a "full democracy," a "flawed democracy," a "hybrid regime," or an "authoritarian regime." Mozambique's low score qualified it as an "authoritarian regime," according to this organization.

The report states, "Sub-Saharan Africa is populated by a large number of 'authoritarian regimes' (encompassing half of the region's 44 countries scored in the Democracy Index). Worse still, the region experienced a significant democratic regression in 2019 ... primarily the consequence of declining score ... in the category of electoral process and pluralism."

Both evaluating reports agreed that the overall state of global democracy was in decline in 2019 and 2020.

and he has the power to dissolve the legislature, call for new elections, declare war, and oversee the military. The president is directly elected by absolute majority vote for a term of five years and is eligible for a consecutive term. Every citizen 18 years or older is eligible to vote.

The prime minister is appointed by the president. He or she presides over the Council of Ministers—the executive cabinet—in which each minister is in charge of specific governmental departments, such as Finance, Transportation, and Education. The prime minister also submits government programs, such as the annual budget, to the assembly.

The Mozambican Assembly is shown here meeting on January 12, 2015.

The legislative branch consists of a one-house (unicameral) parliament, officially called the Assembly of the Republic, or National Assembly. The 250 members are elected by popular vote for terms of 5 years. Of those 250 seats, 2 represent Mozambicans abroad. The other members of the assembly represent Mozambique's 10 provinces plus Maputo, the capital, through a system of proportional representation, in which voters cast their votes for a list of candidates representing political parties or coalitions of parties. The assembly has the authority to veto, or block, some of the president's actions,

City Hall, built in 1947, sits on Independence Square in Maputo.

a power that is balanced by the president's authority to dissolve the assembly before the end of its term. In 2019, the assembly was made up of 151 men and 99 women, with women comprising 39.6 percent of the legislative body.

The judicial branch is headed by the Supreme Court, which is composed of seven justices appointed by the president. The Supreme Court oversees the work of the lower courts.

Local government is in the hands of provincial assemblies in each of Mozambique's 10 provinces and in Maputo, the capital. The executive function is carried out by a governor in each province. Governors are appointed by the ruling national party.

POLITICAL PARTIES

For the first 17 years of Mozambique's independence, the only legal party was the ruling Front for the Liberation of Mozambique (Frente de Liberatacao de Mocambique), or FRELIMO. After the 1990 constitution provided for a multiparty system, 14 political parties took part in the legislative elections. Nonetheless, FRELIMO and the Mozambican National Resistance (Resistencia Nacional Mocambicana), or RENAMO, remain the two dominant parties. Several smaller parties also exist.

DEFENSE

In 1994, Mozambique disbanded its FRELIMO-dominated army as part of the peace process ending the civil war. A new army was recruited from both FRELIMO and RENAMO soldiers. As of 2019, the army numbered about 10,000 troops. There is also a small navy (200 troops) that patrols the coast for poachers and smugglers and a 1,000-member air force. All men and women must register for military service at age 18; there is a two-year service obligation.

In the northern province of Cabo Delgado, the Mozambique Defence and Security Forces face a growing insurgency involving terrorist and militant groups with ties to the Islamic State in Central Africa. The region has rich liquid natural gas deposits. Attacks in the province began around 2017, and by November 2020, the fighting had left around 2,000 people dead and more than 200,000 people displaced. Mozambique hired private military companies based in Russia and South Africa to provide assistance to its security forces.

INTERNET LINKS

www.constituteproject.org/constitution/ Mozambique_2007?lang=en
This is an up-to-date English language version of the constitution of Mozambique.

globaledge.msu.edu/countries/mozambique/government
This site provides a quick overview of Mozambique.

The image of national hero Samora Machel adorns the banknotes of the Mozambican metical.

4

MOZAMBIQUE IS, IN MANY WAYS, A very poor nation. In most assessments of international economic well-being, it ranks as one of the world's 10 poorest countries. Mozambique's colonial history at the hands of Portugal prepared the way for this situation, in the way that colonialism generally does. After independence, further damage was by done by the new government's Communist policies, economic mismanagement, and a brutal civil war from 1977 to 1992.

The civil war, combined with the hostility of neighboring countries, left the nation's economy in ruins. As RENAMO bands raided the country from Rhodesia and South Africa, they destroyed dams and bridges, tore up railroad tracks, and burned villages. Recovery efforts were in full swing when deadly floods in 2000 and 2001 set the country back again. Again, and again, further disasters occurred, most recently with the back-to-back cyclones Idai and Kenneth in 2019, and the COVID-19 pandemic that reached the country in 2020.

That said, Mozambique has great potential. There is plenty of good agricultural land, for example. In fact, about 88 percent of the arable land remains uncultivated. There are also many stands of valuable hardwoods

In 2010 and 2011, deposits of natural gas were discovered off the coast of Mozambique's Cabo Delgabo Province. Ever since, foreign companies have been pouring money into accessing and developing those resources. Mozambique's government hopes the eventual sales of liquefied natural gas will generate revenue and jobs, but critics are skeptical that the impoverished nation will see any benefit at all.

that could provide income for years if harvested wisely. In addition, Mozambique has other natural resources, modern ports, and rail connections to all parts of south-central Africa, while the coast and islands have tremendous potential for tourism.

AGRICULTURE AND FISHING

The nation's economy is based on agriculture. In 2017, about 74.4 percent of Mozambicans relied on farming and fishing to survive, but the agricultural sector accounted for only about 23.9 percent of the country's gross domestic product (GDP).

The major subsistence crops, the crops people depend on for their daily food, include cassava, maize (corn), wheat, and rice, which are grown on the flood plains of the many rivers. This makes them vulnerable to massive flooding,

Workers shell and clean cashew nuts at the Condor Nuts Factory in Nampula, Mozambique.

which occurred in the 2019 disasters of cyclones Idai and Kenneth. Most farms are small, hand-cultivated operations averaging about 3 acres (1.2 ha) in size; there are relatively few commercial farmers. Other crops include cotton, cashew nuts, tea, coconuts, citrus, and sugarcane. Animal production also plays a fundamental role in the lives and nutrition of the rural population.

According to the World Bank, the fishing industry in Mozambique is unstable and underdeveloped. The country's fishing communities are often small, isolated, and poor. Like most of the country's farming, fishing is largely carried out by small-scale subsistence fishers. In 2016, around 65,600 people were working in the fishing industry. A significant number were women, who often fish with small nets, on foot. Women also gather seafood, particularly clams, along the coast.

Some aquaculture has been developed, mostly tilapia and shrimp, but success has been erratic. In 2011, for example, shrimp farming was devastated by an outbreak of a disease called white spot that completely destroyed the stock. Shrimp farms and processing plants closed, and workers were dismissed.

Coal from a mine in Moatize (in Tete Province) is loaded onto a ship at the port of Beira, Mozambique.

INDUSTRY AND MINING

Throughout most of the colonial period, Portugal showed little interest in developing Mozambique's industries out of fear that they would create unfair competition for Portuguese industries at home because of lower labor costs. That changed in 1950, and thousands of Portuguese settlers migrated to Mozambique to take advantage of the emergence of a new business climate. Between 1950 and 1975, industry developed rapidly, focusing mostly on processing sugar, copra (a coconut product), tea, and other agricultural products. One goal of the industrial planners was to provide an array of consumer goods for the growing cities, including beer and soft drinks, radios, and furniture. The only heavy industry was the refining of crude oil.

This industrial base was destroyed in the civil war, and the business owners or managers fled the country. When peace was restored in 1992, the

FRELIMO leaders wisely abandoned their Marxist plans and began a rapid return of businesses to private owners. Businesses that received foreign aid or investment have recovered quickly since. Most of the new industries deal with food processing or the manufacture of furniture and other goods for domestic use.

Today, a mere 4 percent of Mozambique's labor force works in the industrial sector, which includes manufacturing and mining. However, the country has a wealth of metals, natural gas, and coal. Minerals currently being mined include marble, bentonite, coal, gold, bauxite, granite, titanium, and gemstones. Aluminum is the most important metal; Mozambique produces the continent's second-highest amount of aluminium, after South Africa.

In this aerial view, salt mining pans are seen along the shore of Katembe, a suburb of Maputo.

In the late 20th century, vast deposits of coal were discovered in the northwestern Tete Province, and international corporations jumped in to develop mines. One big problem was the lack of transportation infrastructure to move the coal from the minefields to the ports for exporting. Companies had to upgrade existing railroads and construct new ones. In addition, coal storage yards and export terminals needed to be constructed at the ports. Mining finally began in 2011, and the industry continues to grow as more coal deposits are discovered. Meanwhile, however, global demand for coal has been falling as other, cleaner forms of energy production are being developed.

TOURISM

Before independence and the civil war, Mozambique had been a popular destination for tourists. Visitors from South Africa and the landlocked countries enjoyed the beach resorts. Tourism went into a steep decline from 1976 to the mid-1990s. While 292,000 visitors went to Mozambique in 1972, this figure dwindled to about 1,000 each year in the 1980s. By the year 2000, tourism was again the fastest growing sector of the economy.

Gross domestic product (GDP) is a measure of a country's total production. The number reflects the total value of goods and services produced over one year. Economists use it to determine whether a country's economy is growing or contracting. Growth is good, while a falling GDP means trouble. Dividing the GDP by the number of people in the country determines the GDP per capita (per person). This number provides an indication of a country's average standard of living—the higher the better.

In 2017, the GDP per capita (adjusted to purchasing power parity) in Mozambique was approximately $1,300. That figure is extremely low, and it ranked the country at 222nd out of 229 countries listed by the CIA World Factbook. *For comparison, the United States that year was number 19, with a GDP per capita of $59,500; Portugal was number 67 with $30,000; Mozambique's neighbor Malawi was number 223; and the Central African Republic came in last with a GDP per capita of only $700.*

Early in 2000, the Mozambican government created the Ministry of Tourism, which oversees a program called the National Policy of Tourism, setting priorities for the near future. Top priority was given to restoring and expanding the beach resorts near Maputo and Beira. A major rehabilitation project was begun at Gorongosa National Park, the country's most-visited wildlife area.

In 2018, around 2,743,000 visitors arrived in Mozambique, a significant increase from 1,447,000 visitors the year before. The number of jobs in hospitality, catering, travel agencies, and other tourist activities has likewise grown, going from 58,000 in 2015 to 64,600 in 2018. Mozambique still has a long way to go, however, to realize its potential in the tourism sector. Its main assets are its wildlife and natural parks, its many miles of coastal beaches and offshore islands, and its cultural heritage. Music and nightlife, as well as palm-lined sandy beaches and warm tropical waters—surely those are the makings of most tourists' dreams, and the country has plenty to offer.

For example, sport fishing off Benguerra Island is an emerging tourist attraction. Game fish caught in the Bazaruto Archipelago area includes striped marlins, some weighing up to 800 pounds (363 kilograms). Sailfish are caught throughout the year, as are bonito, king and queen mackerel, giant barracuda, and several kinds of kingfish. Experts offer saltwater fishing lessons and demonstrations to tourists, and other specialists give lessons on diving in the waters around the spectacular and unspoiled coral reefs.

However, a vibrant tourism industry requires a robust infrastructure, and in this Mozambique is still lacking. Most tourists expect world-class hotels, restaurants, and transportation facilities. Foreign investment is seen as crucial to this development, and indeed several new luxury hotels and resorts are being constructed as international hospitality corporations bet on Mozambique's future.

INTERNET LINKS

www.cia.gov/library/publications/the-world-factbook/geos/mz.html
The *World Factbook* provides economic statistics about Mozambique.

www.lonelyplanet.com/articles/mozambiques-two-enigmatic-capitals
This travel article looks at Mozambique Island and Maputo from a tourist's point of view.

www.worldbank.org/en/country/mozambique/overview
This organization offers an overview of the country's economic situation.

worldfish.org/GCI/gci_assets_moz/fishing%20and%20aquaculture%20in%20mozambique.pdf
This report provides an overview of fishing and aquaculture in Mozambique.

ENVIRONMENT

Hikers climb up Gorongosa Mountain in Mozambique.

5

LIKE EVERY COUNTRY ON EARTH, Mozambique has environmental problems that need addressing. Wildlife is one of the country's greatest riches, for example, but as people develop and change the environment to their own uses, animals lose more and more habitat. Hunting and poaching add another layer of danger to wildlife species. Another threat is the bushmeat trade—the hunting, selling, and eating of African jungle animals—a tradition that continues throughout the poorest and hungriest parts of Africa. Wildlife, whether protected, endangered, or not, is hunted for food and profit, often using illegal methods and devices that conservationists consider cruel.

Human need also threatens plant life, particularly trees. A great percentage of Mozambicans live in rural areas and use wood for heating water and cooking. Indiscriminate chopping down of trees is adding to the deforestation of the country, but a much larger percent of the forests,

Along with most of southern Africa, Mozambique is especially vulnerable to climate change. With its long coastline, frequent storms, and seasonal flooding, the country is facing increased extreme weather events, natural disasters, hotter temperatures, droughts, deforestation, and sea level rise.

People pick through the huge garbage dump in Maputo.

about 65 percent, are lost to slash-and-burn agriculture. In this form of farming, forests are cut down to create farmland. After a few years, when the soil is depleted, the farmer simply moves on and destroys more forestland. As the forests disappear, animal habitat does as well, and the environmental damage is compounded accordingly.

Agriculture also causes pollution, as poor farming practices impact the environment. Soil runoff washes into rivers and causes sedimentation that runs to the sea, where it affects sea life and corals. Untreated sewage also pollutes the country's waterways, as most communities lack adequate sanitation facilities. Industrial waste and mining effluent—particularly from what is called artisanal (small scale) mining—also pollute the air, waters, and land, and create health hazards. Clean drinking water is not universally available,

especially in rural areas. Similarly, waste management is a growing problem, especially in the rapidly growing cities, where more than 98 percent of collected trash is disposed of at uncontrolled dumpsites.

Environmental issues such as these contribute to widespread public health problems. The widespread lack of sanitation facilities and poor personal hygiene lead to a variety of communicable diseases, which claim thousands of lives every year.

With the help of international aid organizations, Mozambique's leaders and many of its people are working hard to address these issues. They know that the country's economic future can be greatly improved if tourists are drawn to its many wildlife areas. Also, steps are being taken to reduce the environmental causes of illness.

A drilling platform off the coast of Mozambique is evidence of international energy corporations' interest in newly discovered natural gas reserves offshore.

Flamingos take flight on a beach in Mozambique.

WILDLIFE CONSERVATION

The country's civil war was devastating not only to Mozambique's people, but also to its wildlife. Today, the nation's leaders want to restore the country's wildlife areas to their pre—civil war abundance, protect them from poachers, and make them attractive to tourists. It's a monumental and expensive task. Here are some of Mozambique's top national parks.

GORONGOSA NATIONAL PARK   In 2020, Gorongosa marked its 60th year as the country's flagship national park. With more than 1,500 square miles (4,000 sq km), it is located in central Mozambique. Nearby Mount Gorongosa gives the park its name. Great populations of large African mammals—thousands of elephants and hundreds of lions—once roamed its hills and valleys, but today those numbers have been reduced by around 95 percent. The region was hard hit during the long civil war, when fighting in and around the park was almost constant and much of the area was heavily mined. Soldiers killed the zebra, wildebeests, African buffalo, and other animals for food. Both

Tropical Cyclone Idai blew in from the Indian Ocean and hit Mozambique on March 4, 2019. It swept over the land at various rates of force until it finally dissipated on March 21. The storm reached its peak intensity on March 14, at which point it had maximum sustained winds of 120 miles (195 km) per hour. The devastation caused by Idai's winds and rains was calamitous; it was the deadliest storm ever to hit the country. It killed at least 1,303 people in Mozambique, Malawi, and Zimbabwe.

As climate change is expected to bring an increase in such intense storms, Mozambique needs to step up its level of preparedness. Doing so will pose a challenge for the impoverished nation, but not taking the necessary steps will be even costlier. Indeed, Idai was one of the most destructive tropical cyclones in history, causing at least $2.2 billion in damage.

In a report issued in 2020, the World Meteorological Organization identified some of the problems in Mozambique's preparedness and early-warning system, including:

- *an ineffective multi-hazard early-warning system and the fact that people do not understand the terminology used (for example, 50 mm of rain and 150 km/h);*
- *a limited understanding of risks at the institutional, community, and individual levels associated with the absence of hazard mapping (for example, flood mapping for the entire country), exposure and vulnerability assessments, effective land use planning and enforcement for efficient floodplain management;*
- *the absence of effective disaster management plans, including evacuation plans for cities;*
- *problems with the quality and accuracy of warnings, particularly for flooding in some river basins;*
- *building codes that are not suitable to withstand the impact of events of the magnitude of Tropical Cyclone Idai;*
- *the absence of a communication system that can be used in case of failure of normal communication means for warning and emergency operations;*
- *limited emergency response capacities, particularly for search and rescue purposes; and*
- *limited funding to allow meteorology, hydrology, and disaster management institutions to carry out their mandatory functions and to better coordinate with each other.*

The sun sets over Gorongosa National Park in the center of Mozambique.

sides in the conflict slaughtered hundreds of elephants for their ivory, selling it to buy arms and supplies.

In 2004, a restoration project was begun to rebuild the park's infrastructure and restore its wildlife. The elephant population has grown to about 800 from a low of 200 after the war. Where once about 3,500 hippos lived in the 1970s, there are now about 440—up from a mere 100 in 2000. In 2012, there were only 30 to 40 lions in the park, and by 2019, there were at least 146.

As much as progress has taken place, there have been setbacks. Cyclone Idai hit the park in 2019, and in 2020, the park closed completely due to the COVID-19 pandemic.

BANHINE NATIONAL PARK The interior of Gaza Province in southern Mozambique is an arid region, thinly populated, seeming to have very little to offer foreign visitors. However, an interesting experiment is underway at Banhine National Park, a small wildlife area that has received few visitors until now. The park is in the process of joining with several other parks and sanctuaries in Mozambique, Zimbabwe, and South Africa to form the Great Limpopo Transfrontier Park. Fences between the lands have been coming down to allow animals to roam more freely.

The new park, also known as a "Peace Park," was created with the signing of a treaty in 2002. It will cover 13,514 square miles (35,000 sq km) and will be one of the largest in the world.

MAPUTO SPECIAL RESERVE   This small game reserve was hardly known outside Mozambique, although it is only about a two-hour drive from the nation's capital. It was established in 1960 to protect the elephant population in the region. In the 1990s, an American investor had plans to develop a safari business there combined with beach vacations on offshore islands, but he ran out of funds. Since then, poaching has caused heavy damage. Sixty-five white rhinoceroses were introduced into the park from South Africa in the mid-1990s, but all were killed. The number of elephants has been reduced from about 350 in 1971 to fewer than 180 in 1994.

Today, there are more than 400 elephants in the reserve. In addition, more than 4,600 animals of other species have been translocated to the park in recent years, including 8 species that had become extinct there during the civil war. The reserve is part of the newly established Lubombo Transfrontier Conservation Area that is extending across the country to re-establish traditional seasonal migration patterns that have been interrupted by development.

ENVIRONMENT AND HEALTH

One reason that life expectancy is low in Mozambique is that so many people die from diseases that can be controlled or eradicated. As in other African nations, a tragically large percentage of the population suffers from either malaria or AIDS, sometimes both.

Contaminated food and water, as well as poor personal hygiene, contribute to several serious illnesses, such as hepatitis A, typhoid, cholera, and bilharzia (also called schistosomiasis, or snail fever). Through the expansion of local clinics and aid from a variety of international agencies such as the World Health Organization (WHO) and the Bill and Melinda Gates Foundation, rural Mozambicans are learning the importance of avoiding contaminated food or water. One of the most serious challenges is getting protection against infectious diseases.

Efforts are also being made to control the mosquito strains that cause diseases like malaria. While there is no cure for malaria, steps are being taken to drain mosquito-breeding swamps and to make the environment safer. Scientists have found, for example, that sleeping under nets sprayed with a long-lasting insecticide can reduce the cases of severe malaria by 70 percent. The nets cost only a few dollars, but buying and distributing them is not easy in a poor country.

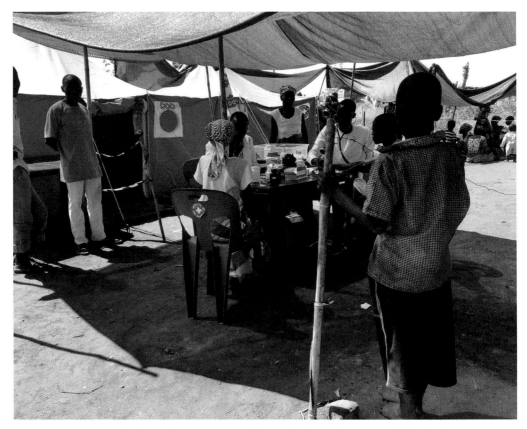

International humanitarian aid workers provide medical services at a site in Beira.

www.fao.org/3/a-bc609e.pdf
This comprehensive publication by the UN's Food and Agriculture Organization is titled "Illegal Hunting and the Bush-meat Trade in Savanna Africa."

gorongosa.org
This is the site of Gorongosa National Park, in English.

news.mongabay.com/2019/12/a-crisis-situation-extinctions-loom-as-forests-are-erased-in-mozambique
This in-depth article examines the deforestation of Mozambique.

www.mozambique.co.za/Mozambique_Travel_Articles-travel/national-parks-mozambique.html
This travel site offers an overview of Mozambique's national parks.

www.nationalgeographic.com/magazine/2019/05/mozambique-gorongosa-national-park-wildlife-rebound
This in-depth article features photos, maps, and graphics about Gorongosa National Park.

www.npr.org/sections/goatsandsoda/2019/12/27/788552728/mozambique-is-racing-to-adapt-to-climate-change-the-weather-is-winning
This article looks as how Mozambique is trying to prepare for the increasing effects of climate change.

www.peaceparks.org
The Peace Parks Foundation has information about the Great Limpopo and the Lubombo Transfrontier conservation areas and their constituent parks in Mozambique.

MOZAMBICANS

Happy children make heart signs with
their hands in Zambezia Province.

6

T HE BITTER CIVIL WAR THAT devastated Mozambique from 1977 to 1992 had a long-lasting effect on the country's population. In addition to the numbers killed or seriously wounded, nearly 2 million fled to other countries. Entire villages were destroyed, and many skilled workers were murdered. Crops were burned and livestock destroyed, along with roads, bridges, and railroads. A generation of young people grew up without schools or clinics and often without families or homes.

Today, Mozambique is a poor, sparsely populated country with a rapidly growing young population. Around 45 percent of the people are younger than 15. This large of a dependent youth population creates a great economic strain on the impoverished country and indicates that more investment needs to be made in schooling and other services for children. However, need alone does not guarantee that the investment can or will be made. Meanwhile, the nation's literacy rate remains quite low, at 60.7 percent, with a large gender discrepancy—in 2017, 72.6 percent of men could read and write; compared to only 50.3 percent of women.

A number of factors contribute to Mozambique's high poverty rate. (In 2015, 46.1 percent of the population was estimated to be living below the poverty line.) Among those factors are recurring natural disasters,

The northwestern and southwestern areas of Mozambique are the least populated. Three large population clusters include: the southern coastal region between Maputo and Inhambane; the central area along the Zambezi River between Beira and Chimoio; and in and around the northern cities of Nampula, Cidade de Nacala, and Pemba.

disease, a quickly growing population, low agricultural productivity, and the unequal distribution of wealth. The country's birth rate is one of the world's highest, averaging around more than 5 children per woman (and higher in rural areas). This ongoing trend typically points to gender inequality, low contraceptive use, early marriages and childbearing, and a lack of education, particularly among women.

Countering the high population growth rate, to some extent, is the nation's high HIV/AIDS and overall mortality rates. Mozambique ranks among the worst in the world for HIV/AIDS prevalence and HIV/AIDS deaths. Complicating that already bad situation, the 2020 global coronavirus pandemic hit the country very hard. As of January 2021, Mozambique had 18,642 confirmed COVID-19 cases and 166 deaths. On September 7, 2020, Mozambique had transitioned from a State of Emergency (SOE) to a State of Public Calamity (SOPC), which triggered increased public safety measures and requirements.

AN ETHNIC PATCHWORK

About 99 percent of Mozambique's people are African. The remaining 1 percent is made up of Europeans (mostly Portuguese), with small numbers of Indians,

Young children play with water from a recently installed water well in a village in the Angoche district of Nampula Province in northeastern Mozambique.

LIFE EXPECTANCY

The best way to assess a nation's general health is by examining certain statistical indicators and comparing them to those of other countries. One of the primary measures used is "life expectancy at birth." This figure is the average number of years a person born in a certain year can expect to live, if mortality factors remain constant. (However, these factors don't remain constant over time, so this statistic is hypothetical.) Since this figure is an average of all life spans within a given framework, it cannot predict any specific person's length of life.

Life expectancy at birth is used to compare conditions in different countries, but it also reflects trends up or down within any given nation. Just as longer life tends to correspond to better overall health in a population, it also aligns with overall quality of life. Therefore, the statistic is valuable in determining, in general, the level of a people's living standards.

In Mozambique, the life expectancy in 2020 was estimated to be 55.9 years; 54.4 years for men and 57.4 years for women. This figure is extremely low, ranking the country at number 222 in the world, out of 228. That means people in 221 nations could expect to live longer lives than Mozambicans, on average. The life expectancy has improved some since 1960, when it was 39.4 years, but it's still a long way from Japan's 2020 expectation of 86 years.

East Asians, and mestiços (people of mixed European and African descent). The African population is divided into more than 200 ethnic groups, with diverse languages, culture traits, and histories.

The basic makeup of the population was established by three historical movements of people. First, in 1000 CE, groups of Bantu people moved into Mozambique from the north and west. Another migration took place in the early 19th century when thousands fled north from present-day South Africa to escape the violent expansion of the Zulu kingdom. Meanwhile, over the past 500 years, Persians, Arab Muslims, Portuguese, and other non-Africans settled along the east coast.

As each new group settled in Mozambique, a basic pattern emerged. The country became divided into two, with the peoples who settled in the north having ways of living quite different from those of the south. The mighty Zambezi River formed the dividing line.

NORTHERN MOZAMBIQUE

Nearly all the ethnic groups in the north live by subsistence farming, although a few also grow some cash crops, while others rely on coastal fishing. Another distinguishing feature of the north is that most societies have a tradition of matrilineal structure—that is, they trace descent through the woman's family line.

The Makua are the largest ethnic group in Mozambique and dominate the north. The Lomwe are another group found in the north, and the Portuguese colonial rulers classified the two groups as one, the Makua-Lomwe, a designation that is still used today particularly in regards to language. Both groups migrated from the upper reaches of the Zambezi and settled between Malawi and the coast along the Indian Ocean.

North of the Makua and the Lomwe are two other large ethnic clusters: the Yao and the Makonde. Both groups straddle the Rovuma River, so they have settlements in Tanzania as well as Mozambique. The Makonde, known for their outstanding wood carvings and masks, have traditionally been one of the most conservative societies—that is, resistant to change. While Muslims managed to convert other ethnic groups to Islam, the Makonde kept their traditional

beliefs. The Yao, who did convert to Islam, now live in the northwest corner of the country. In the 18th and 19th centuries, they were major middlemen in the trade for enslaved peoples and ivory.

Makua women in Pangane wear *musiro*, a traditional white face paint that protects the skin against sun damage.

SOUTH OF THE ZAMBEZI

The Zambezi Valley was settled by a variety of small ethnic groups and also by Portuguese and other non-Africans. Portuguese landowners operated large estates with African workers who were not much more than enslaved peoples.

South of the Zambezi, a number of clans or ethnic groups carved out territory for themselves. These included the Tsonga, Karanga, Shona, Chopi, and Nguni. All were part of eastern Africa's cattle-raising culture. The people lived by farming, but their cattle were the measure of wealth and prestige. The

A woman carries goods to sell on the beach on her head in Barra.

southern societies also differed from the north in being patrilineal—tracing descent through the male line.

The Tsonga, living between the Save River and Delagoa Bay, are the second largest ethnic group in Mozambique. During the years that migrant workers were sent to the gold and diamond mines of South Africa, most were Tsonga. They also form the largest ethnic group in Maputo, the capital. Because so many have worked outside the country and have been exposed to other cultures, they have been more willing than other societies to accept new ideas and change.

Another large group of people, the Shona, forms a majority in Sofala and Manica provinces. The Shona population has been growing because of migrations from South Africa and Zimbabwe.

The many ethnic groups exhibit a spirit of unity in their common desire to build a better Mozambique. There are also similarities in culture, dress, and ways of living. However, each society also retains elements of a separate history and culture. Portuguese colonial leaders discovered how strong those traditions can be when they tried to change traditional agricultural systems in the 1930s. Each group found its own way to resist new systems, and the Portuguese finally gave up.

NON-AFRICAN PEOPLES

The non-African peoples, consisting of Portuguese and other Europeans, Asians, and mestiços, have been few in number, but they have had a powerful influence, especially on the economy.

In 1930, there were only 17,000 whites in Mozambique—nearly all Portuguese. By 1950, the number had grown to about 48,000; this then doubled during the 1950s and reached 250,000 by the time of independence in 1975. The growth of industry and international trade provided incentives for Europeans to come. Many worked in Maputo or Beira, and a small but growing number began building lodges at game reserves and resorts in the beach areas. The Portuguese tried elaborate settlement schemes in the Zambezi Valley, offering Europeans land and agricultural workers, but only a handful accepted the offer.

When Mozambique became independent and the Communist-leaning FRELIMO came into power, the bubble burst. The Portuguese fled almost overnight and, within two years, only 15,000 remained. The flight of the Europeans was devastating to the economy. They had held nearly all the professional and skilled jobs, and many destroyed the facilities they had built rather than see them help a Communist society.

Mozambique is still trying to recover from the chaos created by the departure of the Portuguese and other Europeans. Since 2000, the country's stability and the incentives offered by the government have led to a steady increase in the number of non-Africans in the country. As was the case before independence, most live in Maputo, with lesser numbers in the other cities. British, Germans, white South Africans, Zimbabweans, and even a few Americans have joined the Portuguese in establishing businesses and professional offices. Small numbers of Chinese, Pakistanis, and Indians have commercial establishments, especially along the coast.

SOCIAL STRATIFICATION

Children attend class outdoors under a tree.

In 1927, the Portuguese colonial government established a rigid system of social stratification that continues to influence Mozambican society today. The system divided the entire population into two categories, or classes: the *indígenas* were the indigenous Africans (sometimes called unassimilated Africans), and the *não indígenas*, or nonindigenous, consisting of Europeans, Asians, mestiços, and assimilated Africans, also called *assimilados*. Assimilated Africans were those who had reached a level of "civilization" according to Portuguese standards.

The indígenas, who made up the majority of the population, had few rights. They had to carry identity passes, obey curfews, and pay taxes. They could also be ordered to serve in labor gangs for private business as well as for public works projects.

The não indígenas formed the privileged upper class. They enjoyed full rights of citizenship, and they controlled the economy. Africans could become assimilados by meeting several strict requirements. They had to know the Portuguese language and abandon traditional dress and ways of living. They also had to be employed in industry or trade and provide testimonials of their good character.

Many Africans hated this system that made them second-class citizens. Dislike of the system helped to shape FRELIMO, establishing the goal of creating a society without social classes.

AN EXPERIMENT IN SOCIAL EQUALITY

When FRELIMO came to power in 1975, the movement's leaders were determined to create a classless society, based on the Marxist-Leninist social and economic philosophy that guided Communist nations, particularly the Soviet Union. Mozambique, they declared, would be classless, nonracist, and not ethnically based or segregated by virtue of race. They also wanted it to be an atheistic society.

The FRELIMO idealistic program encountered huge obstacles. The leaders did not take into account the diversity of the people or the strength of their traditions. People in many ethnic groups resisted the attempt to create large state-managed farms. Another program, the setting up of farm collectives in consultation with farm workers, was also difficult because, in most societies, the people were accustomed to having the chief make the decisions on behalf of the community. Many people also disliked the effort to close churches and mosques and to reduce the influence of traditional African religions.

In 1990, FRELIMO leaders agreed to end their experiment with Communism. This move restored traditional chiefs to their positions as the managers and decision makers of their communities. Spiritual leaders also resumed their customary roles and authority.

INTERNET LINKS

www.globalsecurity.org/military/world/africa/mz-people.htm
Mozambican population, demographics, ethnicity, and cultural topics are discussed on this page.

www.mozambique.co.za/About_Mozambique-travel/mozambique-people-faq.html
www.mozambique.co.za/africa_tsonga.html
These two pages on a Mozambican travel site provide short discussions about various ethnic groups.

worldpopulationreview.com/countries/mozambique-population
This site offers population statistics and related information.

LIFESTYLE

A woman opens a coconut with a machete on the beach in Barra.

7

A PERSON'S LIFESTYLE IN Mozambique is largely a matter of location—north or south; farm, village, or city; coast or inland. Access to electricity, clean water, sanitation facilities, medical care, transportation, the internet, and so forth varies considerably between urban and rural areas. People who live far from the cities tend to have fewer resources. Overall, however, most Mozambicans are affected in some way by the country's widespread poverty.

About 63 percent of Mozambique's people live in the countryside, mostly engaged in subsistence farming, very much as their ancestors had been for centuries. The typical farm village consists of several houses clustered around a cattle *kraal* or a meeting place, such as a school. Fields of crops are scattered outside the village. In some societies, each family tends its own plots of farmland; in others, all the families work together and share the harvest.

Small cities, most of which began as trading centers, have grown slowly. Maputo, by far the largest city, has been the country's capital only since the late 19th century. City growth was hampered by Portugal's lack of interest in industry until the 1950s and 1960s. When the Europeans fled after independence, Maputo and other cities became hollow shells,

In 2017, Mozambique decriminalized same-sex relationships, which made it one of the most LGBTQ+-friendly African nations. Although same-sex marriage is not yet legal, the topic appears to be slowly gaining acceptance in public opinion. Nevertheless, discrimination based on sexual orientation is widespread in the country, and there are few or no legal provisions against it.

and some suffered heavy war damage. Since the fighting ended in 1992, cities have become growing centers of business and entertainment.

LIFE IN MAPUTO

Maputo, the bustling, fast-growing capital of Mozambique, is situated on a low bluff overlooking Maputo Bay. With a population of around 1 million people, it is also the capital of one of the smallest but most densely populated provinces in the country. Located at the very southern tip of the country, it lies closer to the borders of Eswatini and South Africa than to much of Mozambique.

Maputo is a busy and attractive port city located where three rivers flow into the Indian Ocean. The growing economy provides an upscale lifestyle for middle-class office workers and store managers. Many city dwellers live in apartment buildings on broad avenues lined with jacarandas, flame trees, and several kinds of palm trees.

Red roofs are a colorful sight in a residential area of Maputo.

The city began as a fishing village around 500 years ago. In the 18th and 19th centuries, the city was named Lourenço Marques, and it was known as the "playground of the rich." With the landlocked gold and diamond regions of South Africa and Southern Rhodesia only 70 to 80 miles (113 to 129 km) away, "LM," as it was called, was a natural destination for good food and lively entertainment. Today, it is a thriving business center and still an important port, presently undergoing some modernization.

Freshly painted office buildings, apartments, restaurants, and stores can be found in most parts of Maputo. In the main business district, called the Baixa (downtown), businesspeople in Western-style clothing talk over lunch or drinks at tree-shaded outdoor cafés. Well-to-do shoppers, many driving Mercedes or BMWs, visit designer shops or the Mercado Central (Central Market), a noisy, lively hodgepodge of stalls selling fruits and vegetables, housewares, and local

A street scene shows a mix of architectural styles in Maputo.

crafts. The pace is easygoing and relaxed, except at night when pubs, bars, and clubs rock with all kinds of music—Western, Asian, and African—until close to dawn. Attractive residential avenues, lined with houses and apartment buildings, overlook the harbor and bay.

The "old town," closest to the harbor, seems even quieter and more laid back than the business district and includes many historic buildings. The huge 1910 railroad station attracts many foreign visitors, drawn to the dome designed by Gustave Eiffel, the French architect famed for his Eiffel Tower in Paris. Nearby are the city's oldest mosque and a modern Roman Catholic cathedral. Another Eiffel-designed structure is known as the Iron House. It was intended as a residence for the colonial governor, but the metal walls held in too much of the tropical heat, so the building has been used primarily as a tourist attraction.

Vibrant though the capital may be, there is a good deal of poverty. Some of the poor live in high-rise buildings left over from the FRELIMO era, when the government built monolithic buildings like those in the former Soviet Union. Since few people chose to live in those structures, they became tenements for the poor. Other poor families have built shantytowns on the outskirts of the city.

OTHER CITIES

During the colonial period, Portugal invested heavily in roads and railroads to connect coastal ports with the interior and with the prosperous mines and towns of South Africa and Southern Rhodesia (now Zimbabwe). As a result, most of Mozambique's cities developed in the south. Transportation connections to the north are, on the other hand, slow and less modernized.

Matola is technically the country's largest city but is essentially a suburb of Maputo. Together, the two cities form the Maputo metropolitan area, with a combined population of almost 3 million.

Beira, Mozambique's fourth-largest city, had the reputation of being a tough seaport town. It had begun as a fishing village in the ninth century, and the modern city was not built until after 1880, upon the completion of the transportation corridor. By 1900, it was a rough-and-tumble port with 4,000 people and 80 bars. It was a major port in the gold trade.

Today, Beira appears rather tired and rundown, but this city of 570,000 has improved considerably over the past decade. The center of the city is being restored, and people can once again meet at attractive outdoor cafés. In the business district, street vendors offer snacks, craft items, and gifts. Beira still has a long way to go to restore the charm of its past. Much poverty remains, and poor people have built shantytowns in the outskirts. Public health, sanitation, and other city services are still in disrepair, but there is hope that foreign investment can speed up the reconstruction.

Public gardens give the city a pleasant, parklike appearance. This is most welcome when the winds off the Indian Ocean turn hot and sticky. A few miles away is the site of the ancient gold-trading town of Sofala. It was once a thriving middle point in the coastal trade, with links to the Persian Gulf kingdoms as

These thatched roof homes in Nampula are typical in rural areas.

FOOD INSECURITY AND MALNUTRITION

Mozambique has a serious hunger problem, according to the 2020 Global Hunger Index, which measures and tracks hunger in countries worldwide. Extreme poverty is the main cause, as most people—80 percent according to this report—cannot afford to eat a sufficiently nutritious diet. Children in particular suffer as a result, and around 42.3 percent of children under 5 are said to be stunted from malnutrition.

The situation used to be worse, greatly exacerbated by the civil war. In 2015, the Mozambican government met its Millennium Development Goal of reducing the number of hungry people by half. However, natural disasters hamper progress. In 2019, the country suffered from both drought and floods, and cyclones Idai and Kenneth ravaged the central and northern parts of the country. The storms ruined crops and farmland and destroyed homes and infrastructure. In addition, increasing terrorist activity in the northern provinces further disrupts society and prevents institutions from helping hungry people.

Numerous international aid groups work in the country to help combat this problem. Education is also needed to help people understand that adequate nutrition is more than simply preventing hunger. Diets heavy in cornmeal or cassava mush may alleviate hunger pains, but they provide insufficient nutrition, particularly for growing children. One program offered by the UN's Food and Agriculture Organization (FAO), for example, teaches women how to grow home gardens to enrich their families' diets.

well as to India and Indonesia. Sofala has since disappeared, although stones from its fort were used to build the Roman Catholic cathedral in Beira.

Other cities in Mozambique are essentially large towns. These include Xai-Xai (pronounced Shy-Shy), Inhambane, Quelimane, Angoche, Namaacha, and Nampula. Nampula is the country's third-largest city and the commercial center of the north. It is the capital city of Nampula Province in northeastern Mozambique and has a population of about 743,125. It is a pleasant, bustling city, with a temperate climate and the long, broad avenues that seem to characterize all of Mozambique's cities. Although the town draws few foreign visitors, it does serve as a transportation crossroads for the whole of north Mozambique and for travel between the coast and Malawi.

A woman goes about her daily chores at her home in rural Matola.

RURAL LIFE

Rural families work hard to scrape together a decent living. Much of the hard work falls on the women, including many thousands who were widowed by the civil war. In addition to raising children, the women are the ones responsible for planting the crops, tending them, and gathering the harvest. They also prepare food for storage or for meals. Even the staple foods require hard work. A basic cornmeal mush, called "porridge," for example, takes a long time to prepare, as the corn (maize) needs to be pounded for several hours before it becomes cornmeal. The porridge is then cooked over an open fire.

In spite of the seemingly endless struggle, there is both variety and hope in Mozambique's rural lifestyles. Over the past century, there have been

Villagers in Macomia turn out to greet some visitors.

several efforts to change rural life, but African traditions have proved stronger than plans created by government authorities. In the 1930s, the Portuguese introduced a system called *shibalo* (from a Swahili word *shiba*, meaning "serf"). Rural people were forced to work on large estates, called *colonatos*, growing cash crops such as cotton and tea. By 1960, almost half the country's cropland was controlled by these estates. The reduction in food crops led to frequent famines. Many farm workers fled to Tanzania, where they joined the FRELIMO independence movement.

When Mozambique became independent in the mid-1970s, FRELIMO leaders tried to reform rural life by establishing large, Soviet-style collective farms and state-owned farms. Although farm families now had a voice in farm management, most disliked the system and welcomed the return to traditional villages.

CHILD MARRIAGE

Most traditions are life-affirming and joyous ways to celebrate one's heritage. However, some customs no longer fit with today's ways of thinking. One such tradition is that of child marriage, an arrangement in which one or both of the parties are under 18 years old. Almost universally, it's the bride who is still a girl, while her groom may be a much older man. This practice occurs in many cultures and countries but is particularly prevalent in sub-Saharan Africa. UNICEF, the UN humanitarian agency for children, in alignment with the UN's Convention on the Rights of the Child, considers child marriage to be a human rights violation. For the children involved, such a marriage is usually forced; girls have no say whatsoever.

According to UNICEF, Mozambique has one of the world's highest rates of child marriage. Around 48 percent of females are married before their 18th birthday; 14 percent are married before the age of 15. Article 30 of the Family Code of Mozambique, adopted in 2004, bans marriage before the age of 18. However, this law is widely ignored, particularly in rural areas.

Child marriage is driven by gender inequality and the belief that men and boys are superior to women and girls. The practice tends to go hand-in-hand with poverty and a lack of education. Young girls who are forced to marry usually have to drop out of school and often get pregnant before they are fully grown, which is a serious health risk. Families may choose to marry off a young daughter for several reasons. For an impoverished family, it's a way to reduce the number of mouths to feed, and the girl's father may gain financially in the exchange. Another reason, however, is because marriage is considered to be in the girl's best interest and a way of keeping her safe from harassment and sexual assault. A girl who has been subject to sexual assault is often considered to be a damaged woman, unsuitable for marriage, and a source of shame to the family, even though none of these things are true.

Child marriage prevents a girl from realizing her potential and deprives society of her potential productivity, intellect, creativity, and leadership. A child bride must put an end to her education. Her job, then, for the rest of her life, will be to care for her husband and mother-in-law, in complete obedience. Giving birth at a young age, which is a typical outcome of this tradition, often damages a girl's body, which has not finished growing.

In partnership with the UN, Mozambique has committed to eliminate child, early, and forced marriage, but changing minds and long-standing customs is no easy task.

REGIONAL VARIATIONS

Geography has had a strong influence on rural ways of living. The differences are especially marked between north and south.

Northern Mozambique has the most densely populated rural areas, including the provinces of Nampula, Niassa, and Cabo Delgado. The entire region is one of great scenic beauty. The coast has picturesque beaches and beautiful offshore islands. The interior coastal plain rises in the west to the cool breezes of the Lichinga Plateau and scenic Lake Malawi. Although the northern three provinces have nearly 40 percent of Mozambique's population, Niassa Province has the lowest density of any province. Historians have concluded that the small population is the result of three factors: years of raids that resulted in the enslavement of thousands of people every year; a long period of endemic sleeping sickness transmitted by tsetse flies; and infertile soil.

Ethnic traditions and location have made it difficult to introduce new ways of living or farming. The Makonde, for example, have always preferred their traditional patterns of subsistence farming. In addition, the north has been quite isolated from Maputo. North-south roads and railroads have been developed only in the past few years, and there were few radios until recently. New farming ideas and techniques could not be introduced in written form because fewer than 10 percent of the people could read or write.

Farming is more productive in central Mozambique, especially in the Zambezi Valley, and in coastal regions throughout southern Mozambique. Good soil and sufficient precipitation have contributed to more intensive vegetable farming. Fields of manioc (cassava) and corn provide two staples, while rice, sugar, tea, and citrus plantations provide important income.

Farm markets with abundant goods in Maputo, Beira, and other urban centers can create the impression that food production is not a problem in Mozambique. Inland from the coast and the river valleys, however, the climate is drier and the land less fertile. In large areas of Sofala, Manica, Tete, and Zambezia provinces, the land is hilly and dry, with baobab trees dotting the landscape. Farms here are spread out, and families struggle against drought, poverty, and disease.

Even in the poorest areas, there has been a slow but steady improvement in the people's standard of living. The government has encouraged the creation of agricultural associations, allowing rural people to work together to improve conditions.

ISLAND AND COASTAL LIFESTYLES

The Indian Ocean coast and the dozens of offshore islands provide a totally different dimension of Mozambican ways of living. The most developed area in terms of tourism is Inhambane Province in the south, which has miles of sandy beaches dotted with palm trees. The calm, clear waters of the Indian Ocean invite a variety of water sports, including fishing, sailing, scuba diving, and snorkeling.

Along the country's coast, several thousand Mozambicans work at beautiful resorts in a wide variety of jobs, from concierge services and kitchen help to managerial positions. In addition, many live in old coastal or island villages such as the town of Inhambane. Like other coastal and island communities,

A resort on Benguerra Island boasts an idyllic view off the Mozambican coast.

Over the past 40 years or more, acquired immunodeficiency syndrome, or AIDS, has had a devastating effect on sub-Saharan Africa. The deadly disease, or spectrum of diseases, is caused by the contagious human immunodeficiency virus, or HIV. (In short, HIV is the virus; AIDS is the disease it causes.) This virus originated as a mutation of the similar simian immunodeficiency virus (SIV) found in chimpanzees and monkeys. In 2006, scientists determined that HIV originated in a community of wild chimps in southern Cameroon and was first passed to people hunting those animals in the 1920s.

Mozambique's first case of HIV was reported in 1986 in the Cabo Delgado Province. By 1999, HIV/AIDS had become the leading killer of people in Africa. Such an enormous loss of life reversed whatever progress many African countries had made in building independent governments and functioning economies after the era of European colonialism ended. As the outbreak grew through the 1990s, millions of children were orphaned or infected with the virus themselves. Huge swaths of the adult working population were enfeebled or wiped out by the epidemic, leaving behind severely weakened communities. By 2010, AIDS had killed more than 15 million Africans.

Although the incidence of HIV/AIDS is slowing, it is far from eliminated, particularly in sub-Saharan Africa. Antiretroviral drugs now exist that slow the progression of the virus in the body, but not everyone who needs them receives them. In 2019, approximately 2,200,000 Mozambicans were living with HIV—about 15.2 percent of women and 9.5 percent of men. Around 150,000 children were living with the infection, and there were more than 1 million orphans due to AIDS. At that time, about 60 percent of infected Mozambicans were receiving the antiretroviral medications they needed.

Inhambane was a thriving town long before the Portuguese arrived. In the 10th century, Muslim ships plied the coast, and, by the 17th century, it was a major port in the trade for enslaved peoples and gold from the interior. Today, some villagers make a living offering tours of the many ancient buildings, including a Roman Catholic cathedral.

Another community with both historical and resort possibilities is the Island of Mozambique (Ilha de Moçambique). This northern island began as a boat-building center about 1,000 years ago and soon established trade ties with Persia, Arabia, and India. The fort of São Sebastião served as the capital of Portuguese East Africa until the late 19th century, when the capital was transferred to Maputo. The fort is still a major tourist attraction. It is the oldest European fort south of the Sahara, and tourism provides work for many of the 14,000 residents. The island was declared a UNESCO World Heritage Site in 1991 because of its beautiful buildings, many of which date to the 16th century. Most of the historic buildings are located in the northern part of the island, while the majority of the residents live in reed houses in the south.

WOMEN

The constitution of Mozambique guarantees equal rights for men and women. Without vigorous government enforcement, however, such admirable ideals exist on paper only. In reality, Mozambican women experience economic, educational, health, and social discrimination. According to several international reports on gender equality, Mozambique ranks among the most unequal countries in the world when it comes to gender. In 2018, it ranked 142nd out of 162 countries in the UNDP's Human Development Report Gender Inequality Index. Low levels of education, high maternal health risks, pressure to marry at a young age, limited economic prospects, gender-based violence, and accepted cultural norms all work together to put women at a great disadvantage. Aggravating the problem, the media often reinforces negative stereotypes by portraying women as deserving of violence. In addition, women suffer greater health problems. For example, HIV infection is higher in young women and adolescent girls than in men and boys of the same age.

EDUCATION

With a large and growing population of children and free education for all mandated by the constitution, Mozambique is under great pressure. Education suffered a serious setback from the civil war, as did most areas of life in Mozambique. More than 5,700 schools were closed throughout the 1980s. By the mid-1990s, less than 30 percent of the local population was literate.

The education record of Portugal's colonial government was a poor one. Since more than 95 percent of Mozambicans were considered second-class

citizens, schooling was ignored or even suppressed. As a result, only 10 percent of the people were literate in 1975 when Mozambique won its independence. The FRELIMO government launched a literacy campaign for children and made education compulsory for ages 6 to 12. Government leaders also hoped that the collective farms would promote education and increase literacy.

The civil war ended the FRELIMO campaign, and schools remained open only in towns that escaped the fighting. In the years since the conflict ended, though, Mozambique has renewed the ambitious literacy campaign. By 2005, the literacy rate for people over the age of 15 had risen to about 50 percent. In 2020, it was up to 60.7 percent.

While elementary school enrollment in the second decade of the 21st century was quite high (statistics vary, but it seems to range from 89 percent to 100 percent), looking beyond those statistics has been more troubling. The World Bank reported that only 19.3 percent of Mozambican children were enrolled in secondary school in 2015. The figures are even worse for girls. According to a report by USAID, more than half of girls drop out of school by fifth grade, and only 11 percent attend secondary school. A miniscule 1 percent of girls continue on to college. Even those children who stay in school do not necessarily receive an adequate education. A lack of qualified teachers, insufficient classroom space, and a shortage of supplies severely hinder the learning process.

There are 11 institutions of higher education in the country. The largest and oldest is Eduardo Mondlane University in Maputo, founded in 1962. This public institution has 30,000 to 35,000 students and offers advanced degrees. Pedagogical University is a public teacher's college in Maputo, with branches in five other cities. There are also several private colleges, including Catholic University of Mozambique in Beira, founded in 1997.

INTERNET LINKS

www.fao.org/fao-stories/article/en/c/1099430
This article discusses nutrition education for women in Mozambique.

www.girlsnotbrides.org/child-marriage/mozambique
Girls Not Brides focuses on child marriage.

notesfromafrica.wordpress.com/2011/05/17/daily-life-in-mozambique-hardship-and-happiness
This short photo essay includes photos of everyday life in Mozambique.

RELIGION

The Roman Catholic Cathedral of Our Lady of the Immaculate Conception shines against a blue sky in Maputo.

8

The constitution
of Mozambique
guarantees freedom
of religion, and
the government
generally abides by
this. Most Muslims
live in the northern
part of the country,
while Christians
dominate in
the south.

N A COUNTRY MADE UP OF AROUND
200 distinct ethnic groups and more than
40 languages, it is hardly surprising that
religion in Mozambique is characterized
by remarkable diversity. According
to 2019 census data, 57.6 percent of
Mozambicans are Christians. That figure
breaks down as follows: 26.2 percent
Roman Catholic, 15.1 percent Zionist
Christian, 14.7 percent Evangelical/
Pentecostal, and 1.6 percent Anglican.

Another 18.3 percent of the people are Muslim—though Islamic
leaders often quote figures of 25 to 30 percent—and 4.7 percent are
either Jewish, Hindu, or Baha'i. The remaining 13.4 percent did not list a
religious affiliation. It's safe to say that many or most of those practice
some form of traditional African religion, which was not included on
the census form. According to Christian and Muslim religious leaders, a
significant portion of the population adheres to syncretic beliefs, that
is, a blend of two unrelated religions. In this case, Christians or Muslims
may also incorporate indigenous, animist beliefs into their faiths.

In the eighth century CE, Muslim traders brought Islam to the coastal regions and offshore islands, and today, almost 20 percent of the people in Mozambique are Muslim. Christianity was introduced by the Portuguese in the 16th century, and missionaries converted some societies or clans to the Roman Catholic faith. Protestant missionaries arrived in the late 19th century, and they continue to be active in the country. Evangelical churches have been working vigorously in recent years to gain new converts, especially among people under the age of 35.

TRADITIONAL BELIEFS

Many Mozambicans who belong to a Muslim mosque or a Christian church mix elements of traditional animism into their beliefs. For example, some people believe that the spirits of dead family members can influence their lives; this faith enables them to add traditional ceremonies or prayers to the Christian belief in an afterlife.

All traditional Mozambican religions are animist—following the belief that every living thing possesses a spirit. In some, there is also the conviction that

A large gathering of people pray together on a beach in Mozambique.

SPIRITUAL HELPERS

In addition to healers, people in many ethnic groups also rely on individuals who seem able to help them in mystical ways. Some are called profetas *(in Portuguese), or spirit mediums, and others are known as* feiticeiros *(in Portuguese)—witch doctors or sorcerers. The profetas might seek a solution to a problem, such as avenging a wrong done or avoiding an illness, by conjuring up the spirit of a deceased family member or an ancestor. In many traditional religions, people believe that the spirits of the dead live on and can influence the daily affairs of the living.*

The fieticeiros use a great variety of techniques, such as charms or casting spells, to help members of certain ethnic groups. Whether the individual is seeking a job promotion, trying to win the affection of another, or seeking revenge for a wrong done, the feiticeiro will intervene. Both feiticeiros and profetas are constantly in demand.

inanimate objects, such as trees, clouds, or lakes, also have spirits. Because these spirits can influence one's life, people take steps to please the spirits or to avoid angering them. The appeasement act might be a prayer, a ritual, a sacrifice, the carrying of a charm, or some other customary practice.

The practices of traditional religions, which have existed for several thousand years, vary considerably from society to society, but nearly all of these include some form of a healer. These faith healers are called *curandeiros* in Portuguese. Many combine ancient practices with modern Western medicine. A curandeiro might first treat a sick person with ancient herbal remedies combined with a healing ritual and then dispense modern pharmaceuticals, such as pain relievers or an anti-inflammatory drug. In many rural areas, this may be the only medical treatment available.

VARIETIES OF CHRISTIANITY

Throughout the colonial period, Roman Catholic missionaries enjoyed a favored position. They were especially active where the majority of Portuguese lived—in the south around Maputo and in the Zambezi Valley. Today, most of Mozambique's Catholics still live in these two areas. Catholics have built elegant

cathedrals in Maputo and Beira, as well as beautiful churches in several cities.

Many Protestant churches and splinter groups have been active since the late 1800s. The larger, well-established churches, such as the Presbyterians, Seventh-Day Adventists, and Baptists, gained converts throughout the 20th century, especially in urban areas.

In recent decades, a number of smaller, lesser-known churches have multiplied. Some of these churches are led by charismatic individuals who prove particularly popular with young people. Services may be simple and informal and are likely to be held in someone's home or a community center. Other small Protestant groups have been built around international peace movements. These became especially popular during the civil war.

ISLAM IN MOZAMBIQUE

In many communities on Africa's east coast, all activity comes to a stop five times a day for the conducting of Muslim prayers. Islam was founded in the seventh century by the Arab prophet Muhammad. The religion spread rapidly, first through the area of the Mediterranean Sea, then eastward across Asia as far as modern-day Indonesia, and south along the African coast and islands. In Mozambique, most of the Muslim population is in the north and along the coast and offshore islands.

Islam today is one of the world's major religions. It is monotheistic, that is, based on a belief in one God, Allah. Muslims share some beliefs of both Judaism and Christianity, such as accepting Abraham and Moses as great prophets. Jesus Christ is also regarded as a prophet, but Muhammad is regarded as the last and greatest of the prophets.

Five pillars, or requirements, form the basis of Islam: professing faith, praying five times daily, giving alms, fasting during the month of Ramadan, and making a pilgrimage to Mecca. The five pillars, as well as obligations such as being honest, just, and willing to defend Islam and prohibitions against eating pork, drinking alcohol, or lending money for interest or gambling, form common bonds among Muslims.

Shown here is a small mosque in Inhambane in the south of Mozambique.

The Five Pillars of Islam are:

1. *Shahada* (sha-ha-DAH): Professing faith in the form of a recitation— "There is no God but Allah, and Muhammad is his prophet."
2. *Salat* (sal-AT): Praying five times a day in the correct manner.
3. *Zakat* (za-KAAT): Giving alms to the needy or to good causes.
4. *Saum* (SOWM): Fasting between sunrise and sunset for the 28 days of the Islamic month of Ramadan.
5. *Hajj* (HAJ): Making the pilgrimage to Mecca at least once in a lifetime.

Five hundred years ago, the Roman Catholic Church and the rulers of Spain launched the Inquisition—a campaign to eliminate nonbelievers from Catholic countries, meaning Jewish people as well as others. This often-ruthless program, which sometimes included torture and execution, spilled over into Spain's close neighbor, Portugal. Many Portuguese Jews fled to Portugal's new territories in eastern Africa.

The Portuguese Jews established a small community on Mozambique Island and later in Maputo. The Jewish community grew during World War II, when many European Jews frantically escaped from Nazi Germany's genocide against all Jews.

Throughout their history in Mozambique, many Jews had to practice their religion secretly. Many sent their children to Christian schools. When the FRELIMO government came to power in 1975, the Jewish synagogues were closed, and the Jews became even more invisible. When religious freedom was established again in the early 1990s, the small Jewish minority was able to practice their faith more openly than it ever had in the past.

While Muslims in the coastal regions of Mozambique are devout, most do not follow the rules of Islam quite as strictly as Muslims in other countries.

ISLAMIST INSURGENCIES

In recent years, an insurgency of extremist Islamist militants emerged in northern Mozambique, particularly in the province of Cabo Delgado. Although some of the militants are native Mozambicans, they are also made up of—and influenced by—outside agitators. Some of these are foreign nationals from Tanzania and Somalia.

The insurgents claim that Islam as practiced in Mozambique has been corrupted and needs to be corrected and purified. To that end, the insurgents have aligned with other factions in East Africa and with the larger Islamic State of Iraq and the Levant (ISIL or Daesh), also known as ISIS, a jihadist group designated a terrorist organization by the United Nations. To accomplish their ends, which include the establishment of a fundamentalist Islamic state and the expulsion of Christianity and other Western influences, the groups began launching terrorist attacks in 2017. By the end of 2020, the attacks had intensified. More than 2,000 people had been killed, 430,000 had been left homeless, and numerous war crimes were alleged against both the rebels and the Mozambican security forces.

INTERNET LINKS

www.globalsecurity.org/military/world/africa/mz-religion.htm
This site provides an overview of religion in Mozambique.

state.gov/reports/2019-report-on-international-religious-freedom/mozambique
The U.S. Department of State reports on religious freedom in Mozambique.

www.voanews.com/extremism-watch/3-years-insurgency-mozambiques-cabo-delgado-remains-vulnerable
This article examines the insurgency in Cabo Delgado.

LANGUAGE

In Pemba, Mozambique, people buy airtime for their cell phones from a roadside shop.

9

PORTUGUESE IS THE OFFICIAL language of Mozambique. A vestige of colonial rule, the language was chosen to be the official tongue at the time of independence because it was ethnically neutral. However, only about 16.6 percent of the population speak it as a first language, and only about half the Mozambican people speak it at all. Far more of the urban population (80.8 percent) is fluent in the language than are people in rural areas (36.3 percent).

Those figures are slippery at best, however, and seem to vary according to source. More important than precise statistics is that most Mozambicans speak more than one language, their own indigenous tongue and another that is deemed necessary for broader communication. Often that is Portuguese, but not always. Swahili, for example, serves as a lingua franca—a language that is adopted as a common language between speakers whose native languages are different—in some parts of the country.

Although more than 40 languages are spoken in Mozambique, along with many dialects, the great majority of the people speak and understand at least one of the eight major African languages. All of the country's

Young children learn to read Portuguese in an elementary school in Manhica. Around 90 percent of Mozambican pupils start school without knowing any Portuguese, the nation's official language.

languages belong to the large Bantu language family. Around 500 CE, the many Bantu people began a great migration from their original homelands in north-central Africa. Over several centuries, they moved south and east. Their languages spread and became increasingly diverse, eventually creating several hundred distinct languages and related dialects.

Knowledge of the country's official language is limited to those who have had at least some schooling. The fact that Portuguese is far from universal creates serious problems because it is the language of business, government, law, and higher education. Mozambicans who have not gone to school, including hundreds of thousands who grew up in refugee camps, have almost no opportunity to advance in those areas.

The government has been trying to upgrade education, including literacy in Portuguese, but the lack of funds has hampered the effort. There are not

English	Portuguese	Swahili
Greetings/Hello	Hola	Salama, Jambo
Good-bye	Até logo	Kwa heri
What is your name?	Como se chama?	Jina lako nani?
		Unaitwa nani?
My name is.	Chamo-me	Jina languni
Thank you	Obrigado.	Asante
Please.	Se faz favor	Tafadhali
	[or] Por favor	
Excuse me	Disculpe	Samahani
	[or] Perdoe-me	
church	igreja	kanisa
mosque	mesquita	misikiti
bank	banco.	benki
river	rio	mto
market	mercado	soko

enough schools or trained teachers. International agencies provide some help, and many schools have started using split sessions, with half the children attending school in the morning, the other half in the afternoon.

REGIONAL LINGUISTIC VARIATIONS

There is no dominant indigenous language, just as there is no dominant ethnic group. Instead, language use is spread geographically, generally corresponding to ethnic groupings.

Students hold up new textbooks in a crowded classroom in a village mosque in northeastern Mozambique.

The eight major Bantu languages can be divided into three major groups. The largest language group is made up of the Makua-Lomwe languages, spoken by more than 30 percent of the population, primarily in the north. The Makonde are Makua speakers, as are the neighboring Yao along the shores of Lake Malawi.

Central Mozambique, especially the Zambezi Valley, has been a meeting place of different groups for centuries, and this is reflected in the languages spoken. A variety of dialects of both the Tsonga and Shona language groups are spoken here, and there are small enclaves of Portuguese.

South of the Zambezi, the majority of the people speak dialects of Tsonga languages, languages that are also spoken in South Africa. The Tsonga language is spoken not only by the Tsonga people but also by the Chopi near the coast. Smaller groups living between the Zambezi and Save rivers speak the Shona language and related dialects. In the extreme south and near the Malawi border are groups who speak Nguni, a language they brought from South Africa when they fled the Zulu expansion of the 19th century.

INTERNET LINKS

omniglot.com/writing/portuguese.htm
omniglot.com/writing/swahili.htm
Omniglot provides an introduction to Portuguese (top URL) and Swahili (bottom).

translatorswithoutborders.org/mozambique-provincial-language-maps
This page has six maps of Mozambique's provinces showing the languages spoken and literacy statistics.

ARTS

Colorful traditional African textiles are displayed
at an open-air market in Maputo.

10

USIC RINGS THROUGH CITY streets, as the sound of drums and guitars fills the air both day and night. It's nearly as common in rural areas, where songs and the rhythms of homemade instruments are woven into the fabric of daily life. Lively dance performances often accompany the music. Along with certain kinds of traditional handicrafts, music and dance are the primary arts of Mozambique.

MUSIC

Traditional music is played throughout the country, but there is a good deal of regional variation in both the kinds of instruments and in the types of music played. In the north, for instance, the Makonde are known for their wind instruments called *lupembe*, usually made from animal horn, although sometimes from gourds or wood. In the south, the *mbila* (plural *timbila*), similar to a xylophone, is the favored instrument of the Chopi people.

In terms of types of music, probably the most popular music in urban areas is known as *marrabenta*. This is lively music, inspired by traditional rhythms, with an irresistible beat that often sounds like calypso, the music of the Caribbean.

Traditional African textiles are decorated with prints of vivid designs. In Mozambique, these boldly patterned fabrics are used in the making of *capulanas*, a type of sarong. The garment is called a capulana, but the cloth itself also goes by that name. Women use the beautifully decorated materials to make dresses, wrap-around skirts, head scarves, and baby carriers.

Marrabenta emerged late in the colonial period. The Portuguese distrusted the folklike rhythms and tried to suppress it, but after independence it resurfaced as the country's favorite music. A band called Orchestra Marrabenta made recordings in the 1980s that spread the music's fame throughout Africa and then the world. Marrabenta has often accompanied performances of dancers from the National Company of Song and Dance. When Orchestra Marrabenta broke up in 1989, some of the band's members formed Ghorwane, which continued to perform in Maputo. By this time, the musical form was known throughout the world as "Mozambican."

By the early 21st century, new individual performers and groups have emerged. Chico Antonio's band, for example, plays melodies based on traditional rhythms, using a combination of bongo drums, flute, and bass, combined with the acoustic and electric guitar. Another member of this new generation of performers is Leman, a trumpet player and former member of Orchestra

A musician in Manica plays a handmade instrument known as a *mbira*.

Marrabenta. Leman mixes traditional rhythms and melodies with various modern sounds.

In southern Mozambique, especially along the coast, the timbila orchestras of the Chopi people provide a contrast to marrabenta. Performed in orchestras of 30 or more, timbila concerts consist of complicated arrangements and dances. Live performances attract large crowds throughout Mozambique and in other countries.

DANCE

Mozambicans are known throughout Africa as outstanding dancers, both in nightclub acts and in traditional theater performances. As in so many elements of the country's life, there are differences between dancing styles of the north and south.

INTANGIBLE CULTURAL HERITAGE

Just as UNESCO works to protect natural and cultural World Heritage sites, it also identifies examples of "intangible cultural heritage of humanity" that need to be preserved. These include, according to the group's website, "traditions or living expressions inherited from our ancestors and passed on to our descendants, such as oral traditions, performing arts, social practices, rituals, arts, festive events, knowledge and practices concerning nature and the universe or the knowledge and skills to produce traditional crafts."

The Convention for the Safeguarding of the Intangible Cultural Heritage has listed two entries for Mozambique: Chopi Timbila, an orchestra of wooden xylophones played by Chopi people in the southern part of the country; and Gule Wamkulu, a ritual dance of the Chea people in Malawi, Zambia, and Mozambique.

A timbila, a traditional Mozambican wood xylophone-like instrument, is played with rubber mallets.

Perhaps the most famous dance style in the north is called *tufo*, first developed on Mozambique Island. Tufo is a rather slow-paced dance probably influenced by Arabic dances. Normally, it's performed only by women, accompanied by special tufo drums. The dancers wear matching sarongs, called capulanas, and scarves, producing an elegant, fluid movement.

In the south, the Chopi people perform a faster-paced dance with the timbila orchestras. The dance, called the *makwaela*, features a cappella singing and fast, intricate foot percussion.

Live dance performances are frequent throughout the country. The House of Culture (Casa de Cultura) in Maputo, for example, is the home of the National Company of Song and Dance. Tickets to the performances are fairly expensive, but rehearsals are usually open to the public at no cost.

LITERATURE

During most of the colonial period, few Mozambicans could read and write Portuguese, and there was no literature in the traditional languages. That began to change when Mozambique's independence movement began. Two of the most famous poets of this early independence movement were Rui de Noronha and Noemia de Sousa. Both poets focused on the themes of nationalist identity and solidarity.

Late in the 1940s, José Craveirinha began writing about the suffering of the people under Portuguese rule and called for a popular uprising. His protests led to his arrest and imprisonment. Freed after independence, Craveirinha is today regarded as one of Mozambique's greatest writers. His work, including *Poem of a Future Citizen*, is well known throughout the world. Another nationalist writer and a contemporary of Craveirinha—Luis Bernardo Honwana—was famous for his powerful short stories, including *We Killed Mangey Dog* and *Dina*.

During the struggle for independence, freedom fighters in the FRELIMO movement began writing about their lives and encounters. They wrote stories and poetry about their forest camps, the frequent marches, the ambushes, and the gun battles. Marcelino dos Santos was probably the most famous of these "guerrilla poets."

MAPIKO: A RITUAL DANCE

A traditional dance of the Makonde people is called the mapiko. *It probably originated several centuries ago as a ritual designed to ensure men's dominance over women. The male dancer wears a special wooden mask (*lipiko; *plural* mapiko*), pictured here, which is decorated with dyes, pictures, and hair. His clothing is made from five pieces of cloth that cover him completely except for his hands and feet. The dancer represents the spirit of a deceased person, and the ritual is choreographed to frighten women and young children,*

convincing them that only the men of the village can protect them from the spirits of the dead. The dance is performed in the late afternoon and must be completed by sunset.

After independence was achieved in 1975, writers and poets felt more literary freedom from government interference, although censorship was used by FRELIMO during the conflict against the RENAMO rebels.

New Mozambican writers emerged during the 1990s, including Mia Couto, whose works include *Voices Made Night* and *Tale of the Two Who Returned from the Dead*. Other famous writers of the period are Ungulani Ba Ka Khosa, Lina Magaia, and Eduardo White. A more recent international sensation was Farida Karodlia's *A Shattering of Silence*, a tale of a young girl's journey through Mozambique after the death of her family.

PAINTING

The most famous painter in Mozambique was Malangatana Valente Ngwenya, known as Malangatana. His powerful art detailed the sufferings of the people

during the colonial period and the civil war years. Malangatana's paintings have been exhibited in galleries around the world.

An artist displays his paintings for sale on a street in Maputo.

Another well-known artist was Bertina Lopes. Her work emerged from her research into the themes, colors, and designs of ethnic art and crafts. Another artist, Roberto Chichorro, has gained fame for his paintings of childhood memories. Paintings and sculptures of all of the country's artists are frequently exhibited in the National Art Museum in Maputo.

CRAFTS

Among the best known crafts in Mozambique are wood carvings. Beautiful sandalwood sculptures are made in the south, and ebony carvings are produced

by Makonde carvers in the north. The late Alberto Chissano was the most famous sculptor, and his work received international acclaim.

The main center of Makonde wood carving is in Cabo Delgado Province, followed by Nampula. Most carvings depict traditional themes, but a number of artisans are experimenting with more modern styles. Nkatunga is one of the new generation of sculptors producing striking sculptures of rural life.

Mozambique's craft workers are also well known for their ceremonial wooden masks. The masks are popular with international art collectors, who display them as wall hangings.

Basketry and woven mats are other examples of outstanding Mozambican crafts. Palma, located in the north near the Tanzania border, is the unofficial capital of basketry. Most of the crafts are made in outlying villages, then sold at the weekly market in town.

The Saturday morning craft market at Maputo, called the Mercado Artesanato, is another important center for the display and sale of Mozambique's crafts. In addition to wood carvings, baskets, and woven mats, there are batik fabrics and jewelry items crafted from semiprecious stones like malachite. There are also larger items, such as reed chairs, cabinets, and bookshelves.

This entrance to a crafts and food fair is at the city center in Maputo.

INTERNET LINKS

www.apollo-magazine.com/art-diary/malangatana-mozambique-modern
This art magazine site covers the life and work of Malangatana.

www.buala.org/en/stages/tufo-dance-cultural-heritage-of-mozambique
This site describes the tufo dance of Mozambican women.

ich.unesco.org/en/state/mozambique-MZ
Links for Mozambique's Intangible Cultural Heritage listings are provided on this page.

whc.unesco.org/en/list/599
This is the page for Mozambique's one entry on the World Heritage List, the Island of Mozambique.

LEISURE

Children might not have expensive toys in
Mozambique, but they still have fun.

MOZAMBICANS SPEND MOST OF their time engaged in the daily work of earning a living. They have little free time—and even less money—for the pleasurable pursuit of leisure. Nevertheless, they do find ways to enjoy a variety of activities. Women sing as they work in the fields, and children manage to play games. More than half the people live near water, giving them the opportunity to swim or to fish (for pleasure as well as to add to the food supply). Even the poorest enjoy many family activities, including celebrating birthdays, weddings, and holidays. Quite a few people own bicycles, but these are for transportation rather than recreation.

For Mozambique's growing middle class, as well as for tourists and foreign aid workers, the country's recreation potential is remarkable. Wildlife areas, beautiful cities, coastal regions, and offshore islands offer a wide array of leisure opportunities.

11

Mozambique competes regularly in the Summer Olympics but has never taken part in the Winter Games. The track and field athlete Maria Mutola is the country's only Olympic medal winner as of January 2021. She specialized in the 800-meter running event, winning gold at the 2000 Games and bronze at the 1996 Games. She was also only the fourth athlete to compete in six Olympic Games.

Older children play volleyball for recreation at a school on Benguerra Island.

COASTAL RECREATION

For anyone who has daydreamed about being in a tropical paradise—a place where gentle breezes whisper through palm trees that border white-sand beaches and crystal-clear waters sparkle in the sun—that postcard image is an accurate description of coastal Mozambique. The country measures around 1,100 miles (1,770 km) from north to south, but the many bays and inlets extend the actual coastline to 1,535 miles (2,470 km), plus the coastlines of dozens of offshore islands. Much of the coast is a tropical paradise in its own right.

While many islands and coastal areas are practically uninhabited, other areas are idyllic recreation areas, crowded with visitors on holiday and school vacations. A steadily growing number of Mozambicans enjoy these resorts along with more and more tourists from neighboring countries. Smaller numbers come from Europe, the Persian Gulf States, and India.

Some recreation areas offer special activity opportunities. Scuba diving enthusiasts, for example, flock to resort areas such as Ponta do Ouro, Inhaca Island, and Bazaruto—places where there is a great variety of marine life and coral reefs. Ponta do Ouro is also one of the favorite destinations for those interested in surfing.

The Bazaruto Archipelago offers some of the most challenging game fishing in the world. Large black and striped marlins are a favored autumn catch, and it is not uncommon for a fish to weigh as much as 800 pounds (363 kg). Other game fish include tuna, sailfish, king and queen mackerel, giant barracuda, and several species of kingfish (including the mighty trevall).

Dolphin-watching tours draw people to several offshore islands. Even more popular are dhow safaris, available around the Bazaruto Archipelago and from Iho Island. Dhows are picturesque boats, each with a single tall mast and sail.

Tourists and locals enjoy the turquoise green waters at the beach in Ponta do Ouro, just 6 miles (10 km) from the border with South Africa.

They have been in use for several thousand years and are still a common sight on Africa's Nile River, the Suez Canal, and inland lakes, as well as the coastal waters. Traditional boats could sail only with the wind, but modern dhows are equipped with outboard motors. Families can take a dhow for a day of fishing or diving and enjoy a picnic. More ambitious trips around the islands take from two to four days.

Two activities that draw surprising numbers are bird-watching and shell collecting. Bird enthusiasts come from as far away as Europe and North America for bird-watching safaris. All are invited to contribute to the Mozambique Atlas Bird Project—an effort to catalog all of the country's birds, including some that are extremely rare, such as Eleanora's falcon and the stripe-breasted canary. Bird-watching centers include seaside regions such as the Bazaruto Archipelago and inland areas such as Gorongosa National Park.

Experts say that Mozambique's coastal areas and islands constitute one of the best regions in the world for shell collecting. Almost every type of shell found in the Indian Ocean and as far away as the western Pacific washes up on the beaches of Mozambique. Shell collectors from all over the world come in search of rare, or even new, kinds.

ENTERTAINMENT

Mozambique's attractive cities and large towns provide many ways to fill leisure time. People enjoy sitting at sidewalk cafés and observing bustling street scenes. Street vendors and outdoor markets sell handmade baskets, weavings, batiks, and jewelry, as well as fresh fruits, vegetables, seafood, and household goods. An afternoon or weekend stroll takes people through tree-lined streets or "old towns," featuring 16th-century churches and the crumbling stone walls of ancient forts.

The larger cities are also busy at night. Restaurants provide some of the best cuisine in Africa, with Portuguese, African, and Indian influences. Nightclubs, pubs, and clubs offer dancing and many kinds of music, including American jazz and blues. Maputo's popular street fair, called Feira Popular, features amusement-park rides, such as bumper cars, as well as dozens of bars and restaurants.

There is also more sophisticated entertainment, such as Maputo's Casa de Culture (House of Culture), which provides outstanding performances by the National Company of Song and Dance. The Teatro Avenida offers performances by local theater groups, usually in Portuguese. Movie houses show fairly recent American and European films in their original language with Portuguese subtitles.

Mozambicans and visitors to the country can enjoy a surprising number of museums. Maputo has an excellent National Art Museum as well as the Natural History Museum and the Museum of Geology that provide interesting information about the country. In addition, the Money Museum offers a history of currency, including early forms of barter.

Students play chess in pairs at a secondary school sports festival in Manica.

In rural areas, dance is the favorite form of entertainment, and every ethnic group has its own unique dance style. The Chopi people in the south continue to perform an ancient hunting dance. The performers wear lion skins and carry long spears and large oval shields. The music is similar to Caribbean calypso.

In north-central Mozambique, the Makua men perform a lively dance on stilts, making their way around a village to the great delight of their audience. The women of Mozambique Island also combine dance with athletic skill in a dance that includes jumping rope to a fast beat.

People also play traditional board games, including the national favorite, butterfly. The game, which is something like checkers, is named for the design of the board, which resembles the wings of a butterfly. Another popular game is *ntchuva*, which is similar to mancala. It requires no special equipment, as it can be played in the sand, using small stones, or it can be played on a wooden game board.

High school girls play football (soccer) in Manica.

SPORTS

Mozambicans enjoy a variety of Western-style sports. Many hotels provide gymnasiums and swimming pools, available to city residents as well as hotel guests. Maputo has public tennis courts in the Botanical Garden, and there is a golf course just outside the city.

The most popular sport in Mozambique is soccer (known as football outside the United States). Boys and girls throughout the country play whenever they can. Some villagers even use a homemade ball made of rags or animal bladders if a real ball is not available, and two or four sticks serve as goals. Beaches often serve as playing fields. Throughout the country, semiprofessional teams play matches in packed stadiums, including Machava Stadium in Maputo, which seats 60,000 spectators. The newer Zimpeto Stadium, which opened in 2011, holds 42,000 spectators. It now serves as the home field for the national football team.

The Mozambique national team has performed well in international competition but has never qualified for the FIFA World Cup. On several occasions, most recently 2010, the team has represented the country in the Africa Cup of Nations, though it has never made it to the finals.

INTERNET LINKS

www.olympic.org/maria-mutola
The Olympics website has a page that focuses on the Mozambican athlete Maria Mutola.

www.photodestination.co.za/mozambique-birding.html
Birdwatching in Mozambique is the topic of several essays on this site.

www.thesprucecrafts.com/games-played-in-africa-1454491
This list of traditional African games includes butterfly and mancala.

FESTIVALS

A teenager in Maputo celebrates the 40th anniversary of Mozambican independence with the nation's flag painted on her face.

12

HISTORY HAS SHAPED MOZAMBIQUE'S festival days, with its struggle against Portuguese rule foremost in the establishment of several important national occasions. Religious holidays are observed but are not accorded public holiday status. The movement for independence and the FRELIMO government's attempts to establish a Communist society led to a decline in religious celebrations, both Roman Catholic and Muslim. Subsequently, after the government's retreat from Communism with the 1990 constitution, the major religious holidays were celebrated again.

Throughout the country, ethnic groups and villages choose their own ways to celebrate public holidays. They also have their own traditional celebrations and festivities. There are several annual music events, the most important being the Azgo Festival in Maputo, which features artists from Mozambique and all of Africa. (The 2020 Azgo fest was cancelled due to the COVID-19 pandemic.)

Women dance and sing dressed in colorful traditional African fabrics to celebrate special days in Mozambique.

NATIONAL HOLIDAYS

The year begins with New Year's Day, as it does for nearly every country. In the cities and towns, people celebrate New Year's Eve with dinners, dances, parties, and a midnight toast. January 1 is the actual holiday when schools, businesses, and offices are closed.

On February 3, Mozambique celebrates Heroes Day, followed by National Day (formerly Independence Day) on June 25, and Victory Day, September 7; all three celebrate the country's independence from Portugal in 1975. Armed Forces Day, also called Revolution Day, on September 25, is a commemoration of the army's role in winning independence and in achieving peace in 1992.

Likewise, October 4 is Peace and Reconciliation Day, which marks the end of the Mozambican civil war.

These patriotic holidays are marked by parades and political speeches. In the late 1970s, these days were also occasions for rallies in support of the Marxist ideals of a society based on complete equality. Three other public holidays— Women's Day (April 7), Workers Day (May 1), and Family Day (December 25)— were also part of the government's efforts to create greater equality. They continue to be celebrated but with far less fanfare than in the past.

There are several other days that the government considers days of commemoration, but they are not official public holidays, meaning that schools, offices, and businesses can stay open. The Day of African Unity is celebrated in large areas of the continent on May 25, and the same is true of International Children's Day on June 1. Two other commemorative days— Resistance Day, June 16, and Assumption of Power by the Transition Government, September 20—celebrate Mozambique's independence. Resistance Day marks the first time FRELIMO fighters took up arms against the Portuguese. The Assumption of Power celebrates the transition to full independence. In addition, each city has its own public holiday. Maputo's day is November 10.

CHRISTIAN HOLIDAYS

When the FRELIMO government took office in 1975, the leaders hoped to follow the Communist ideal of creating a society with no separate social classes and with no religion. Churches, mosques, and Hindu temples were closed, but the government could not make the ban on religion stick. By 1990, the new constitution gave everyone the right to worship. As a concession to Marxist ideals, the constitution also stated that everyone also had the right "not to worship," but the people paid little attention to that and quickly returned to their traditional religious practices.

Mozambique's Christians have special celebrations on Christmas (December 25), Good Friday, and Easter. The dates for Good Friday and Easter change every year but are usually in March or April. Good Friday is always the Friday before Easter Sunday.

Young men from a church group dance and play traditional strap drums in Manica at a celebration.

Christmas festivals are a favorite with nearly every ethnic group because celebrating a birth is an important part of traditional celebrations, and Christmas celebrates the birth of Jesus Christ. Good Friday (honoring the day Jesus died) and Easter (the day Jesus was said to have risen from the dead) also fit in well with traditional ceremonies based on the idea that the spirits of the dead can return to earth and influence people's lives. Not surprisingly, the celebration of these days often includes elements of traditional ceremonies.

ISLAMIC FESTIVALS

Muslim festivals are generally timed according to the lunar calendar. Therefore, the dates differ from year to year. The most important holy period in the Muslim year is the month of Ramadan. During that period, every adult Muslim fasts from dawn until dark every day, following the practice established by the Prophet Muhammad. The faithful can eat from sunset until almost dawn.

Ramadan ends with Eid el-Fitr, a two- or three-day festival during which Muslims gather with family and friends for feasting, praying, and exchanging gifts. It is also customary to go to services in the mosque at the end of the month and also to give generously to the poor. The birthday of Muhammad, the founder of Islam, is celebrated during Mawlid al-Nabi.

TRADITIONAL CELEBRATIONS

Many traditional ethnic and family ceremonies have been replaced by Christian or Muslim practices, but some festivals remain unchanged. Many have rituals revolving around spring planting or a good autumn harvest.

In one Makonde celebration, several men "casually" announce that they have to go away for a few days. While they are gone, villagers prepare for the harvest festival. Suspense builds until one night, when the moon is just right, masked dancers leap into the village, waving torches, chanting, and beating drums. The people rush to join them. Three days and nights of feasting, singing, and dancing follow. When the celebration is over, the missing men return, and the villagers pretend that the masked dancers have disappeared.

INTERNET LINKS

azgofestival.com/en
This is the home page of the Azgo music festival.

www.officeholidays.com/countries/mozambique
This listing has links to explain the Mozambican holidays.

www.timeanddate.com/holidays/mozambique
This calendar site provides a list of annual holidays in Mozambique.

FOOD

Women sell peanut seeds at a fresh market at Vilankulo.

13

MOZAMBIQUE'S CUISINE REFLECTS its long history. Oranges and lemons, for example, were brought from the eastern Mediterranean by Arab traders as early as the ninth century. Some crops came from parts of Asia— rice and sugarcane from Indonesia, tea from China, and mangoes and ginger from India. These foods probably arrived in Mozambique after 1100.

A number of important crops came from the Americas, particularly Brazil and other regions controlled by Portugal during colonial times. These include two of the most important staples, corn and cassava. Peanuts, cashew nuts, and pineapple also came from the Americas and are an integral part of Mozambican cuisine today. The influence of the Portuguese is evident in many dishes, particularly the soft, white bread rolls called *paõ* (pow). The Portuguese introduced onions, garlic, paprika, chili pepper, red pepper, bay leaves, and wine.

Common foods are also influenced by the country's geographical location. Seafood, for example, is plentiful along Mozambique's extensive coastline. Coconuts, avocados, mangoes, and papayas grow in the tropical climate. The cuisine's flavor profile is hot and spicy, with an abundant use of fiery chillies, garlic, and lemon.

Nuts and legumes, including peanuts, are a common part of the Mozambican diet. Women sometimes sell peanuts in the market.

A typical dish of *xima* is served with *piri-piri* sauce.

RURAL STAPLES

Rice, corn, and cassava are the staples in the diet of rural Mozambicans. One or more of these is eaten every day, providing a low-cost dish that is filling. The addition of sauces, fruits, or peanuts adds to the nutritional value.

One popular dish, called *xima* (chi-ma), sometimes spelled *ncima*, is made from maize, or corn flour. Sometimes it is mixed with cassava. The thick, white, pasty food is similar to polenta or grits. Women prepare this porridge-like dish by grinding corn and cassava together, using a wooden pestle and a large, deep wooden bowl. The dish is served in calabashes (hollowed gourds). Roasted peanuts might be added for flavor, along with a weak wine, *utchema*, made of palm leaves. Small chunks of chicken or other meat can also be mixed in.

Xima acts as a base for almost every Mozambican meal. The people often say, "A person who is accustomed to eating xima will only want to eat xima for the rest of his life." However, this porridge lacks essential nutrients and is widely eaten mostly because it holds off hunger. In very poor areas, diets primarily based on xima are nutritionally insufficient, particularly for children.

Matapa (or *mathapa* or *matata*) is a green stew often served with rice or xima. It's made with chopped clams or shrimp, ground peanuts, coconut, seasonings, and greens. Chopped casaba greens are traditional, but other types can be substituted.

Beef and chicken are important sources of protein, but both are expensive, especially beef, so they are served only as a special treat. Many rural families sometimes have chicken, and in the south, beef is not uncommon. Both are likely to be served with *piri-piri*, a very spicy red- or green-pepper sauce that Mozambique is famous for. Chicken is also served in a stew with peanuts and pumpkin leaves. The Portuguese influence is seen in *feijoada*, a hearty bean stew cooked with meat—typically beef, pork, or both. It can also be made with shellfish.

A beef and bean feijoada is a favorite Mozambican meal.

Flavorful foods, such as chillies and ginger roots, are set out for sale at a market in Maputo.

COASTAL VARIATIONS

On the islands and in coastal areas, the abundance of seafood provides a varied menu. Mozambique is famous for its shrimp (*camarões*) and lobster (*lagosta*). These are valuable exports and are also widely used in domestic recipes.

One popular dish is *macaza*, made with shrimp, lobster, or prawns. The shellfish is put on bamboo skewers and grilled over an open fire. *Bacalhao* is a stew made of dried and salted fish mixed with vegetables, and *chocos* is squid cooked in its own ink. Seafood dishes often include coconut, peppers, onions, or special leaves for seasoning. A dish called *mu-kwane*, made of seafood mixed with coconut and cassava leaves, can also be found.

EATING OUT

Rural Mozambicans rarely eat in restaurants, but restaurant dining is popular in the cities. Maputo, Beira, and several larger towns offer a mixture of cuisines—African, Indian, and Portuguese.

Not surprisingly, Mozambique's restaurants are best known for their seafood, often made with a touch of piri-piri. Seafood and chicken are usually served with rice or French fries. Many dishes have a Portuguese influence, often cooked with wine or the fortified wine called port. There are also restaurants serving Indian, Chinese, Italian, and Malaysian food, and most cities will also have a pizza parlor.

There are numerous fast-food places, especially in Maputo. Diners can find American-style hamburgers, Tex-Mex items like burritos or tacos, rolls, pastries, and even quiches.

Beverages include the usual assortment of American and European soft drinks. Tea is the most common drink around the country, and homemade beer is popular too. Fruit juices are also available, and bottled water is increasingly common. Although several plantations grow excellent coffee, it is found almost exclusively in restaurants, rather than in people's homes.

INTERNET LINKS

www.tripsavvy.com/the-top-foods-to-try-in-mozambique-4146959
This travel site provides photos of 10 popular Mozambican dishes.

www.wfp.org/countries/mozambique
The UN World Food Programme discusses Mozambique's chronic food insecurity and other food-related problems.

MATAPA

In place of the usual cassava greens, this recipe uses collard greens. Chard or spinach may be substituted. For a vegetarian version, leave out the shrimp.

1 pound (454 grams) fresh or frozen (thawed) shrimp
4 cups (946 milliliters) water
1 teaspoon salt
2 bunches collard greens (substitute kale, chard, or spinach)
2 13.5-ounce (398 mL) cans coconut milk
1 pound (454 g) raw unsalted peanuts
4 cloves garlic, pressed or finely chopped

Peel and devein the shrimp. Place the shells and 2 cups (473 ml) of water in a large saucepan. Boil for 5 minutes, then strain, reserving the liquid. Set aside.

Remove the tough center ribs of the greens. Place the leafy greens in a food processor, and blend thoroughly. Transfer to a large Dutch oven. Add the reserved shrimp shell liquid, salt, and 1 can of coconut milk. Bring to a boil, lower heat, and simmer for 30 minutes.

In a separate saucepan, boil 2 cups (473 mL) water, add shrimp, and simmer for 5 minutes. Strain and refrigerate shrimp. Return the liquid to the saucepan.

In a food processor, grind peanuts to a powder. Add to the the shrimp broth along with the remaining can of coconut milk. Heat slowly over medium to a boil. Add it to the greens mixture in the Dutch oven; add garlic. Cover, and simmer for 90 minutes. During the final 5 minutes, add the shrimp, and heat through. Serve the matapa over rice or accompanied by xima.

XIMA

Combine 1 cup (240 mL) cold water and 1 cup (160 g) white corn meal. Mix well to remove lumps. Set aside. In a large saucepan, heat 3 cups (700 mL) water and 1 teaspoon salt until boiling. Remove from the heat; whisk in the corn meal mixture until smooth. Return the pan to the heat, and return to a boil, stirring constantly. Cover, turn the heat to low, and continue to cook for 5 minutes. Serves 4.

BOLO POLANA (CASHEW NUT CAKE)

This citrus-scented cake is often served for special occasions.

1 large baking potato, peeled, boiled, and mashed
1 cup (150 g) raw cashews
¾ cup (170 g) unsalted butter, at room temperature
⅔ cup (130 g) granulated sugar
4 large eggs, separated
Zest of one lemon
Zest and juice of one orange
2 teaspoons vanilla extract
½ teaspoon salt
4 tablespoons heavy cream
1 ½ cups (190 g) all-purpose flour
Confectioner's sugar (optional)

Preheat the oven to 350 degrees Fahrenheit (175°C). Spray an 8-inch (20 centimeter) square (or 9-inch round) baking pan with non-stick spray. (Alternatively, butter and flour the pan.)

Place the cashews in the bowl of a food processor, and pulse until finely ground. Set aside.

Meanwhile, in a large bowl, combine the butter and granulated sugar, and beat until fluffy. Add the egg yolks, one at a time, mixing in before adding the next. Whisk in the cashews, lemon and orange zests, orange juice, vanilla, salt, and cream. Using a rubber spatula, stir the mixture to make sure everything is well combined, and then gently fold in the flour and mashed potato.

In a separate bowl, beat the egg whites until they form stiff peaks. Using the rubber spatula, stir a third of the egg whites into the batter to loosen the batter, then gently fold in the remaining egg whites. Transfer the batter to the prepared pan.

Bake until golden and firm, about 1 hour and 10 minutes. Let the cake cool completely in the pan on a wire rack. Turn it out of the pan, and set it right-side up on a serving plate. Sprinkle with the confectioner's sugar, if desired, then cut into wedges and serve.

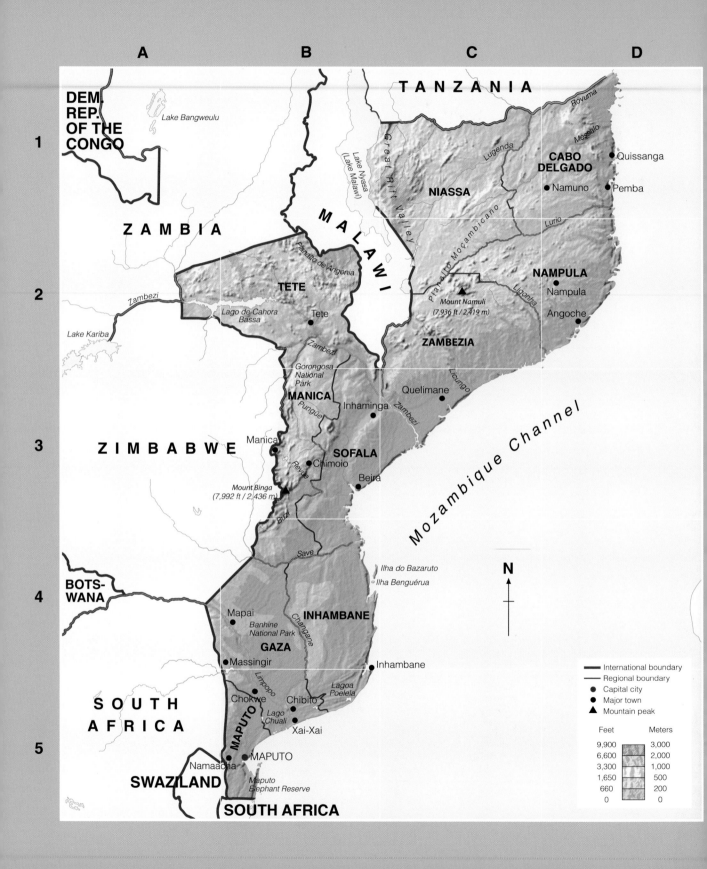

	A	B	C	D

DEM. REP. OF THE CONGO

Lake Bangweulu

T A N Z A N I A

Rovuma

1

Z A M B I A

Lake Nyasa (Lake Malawi)

Messalo

Lugenda

Great Rift Valley

M A L A W I

NIASSA

CABO DELGADO

● Quissanga

● Namuno

● Pemba

Lurio

Planalto de Angonia

2

Zambezi

TETE

Lago de Cahora Bassa

● Tete

Lake Kariba

Zambezi

Planalto Moçambicano

▲ *Mount Namuli (7,936 ft / 2,419 m)*

Ligonha

NAMPULA

● Nampula

ZAMBEZIA

● Angoche

Gorongosa National Park

MANICA

Pungüe

Inhaminga ●

Zambezi

● Quelimane

Licungo

3

Z I M B A B W E

Manica ●

Revue

SOFALA

● Chimoio

Beira ●

Mozambique Channel

Mount Binga (7,992 ft / 2,436 m) ▲

Buzi

Save

Ilha do Bazaruto

Ilha Benguérua

N

4

BOTS-WANA

Changane

INHAMBANE

● Mapai

Banhine National Park

GAZA

● Massingir

Inhambane ●

Limpopo

Lagoa Poelela

S O U T H A F R I C A

● Chokwe

● Chibito

Lago Chuali

● Xai-Xai

MAPUTO

5

● MAPUTO

Namaacha ●

SWAZILAND

Maputo Elephant Reserve

SOUTH AFRICA

▬▬	International boundary
──	Regional boundary
●	Capital city
●	Major town
▲	Mountain peak

Feet	Meters
9,900	3,000
6,600	2,000
3,300	1,000
1,650	500
660	200
0	0

MAP OF MOZAMBIQUE

Angoche, D2

Banhine National Park, B4
Beira, B3
Botswana, A4
Buzi River, B3, B4

Cabo Delgado, C1, C2, D1, D2
Changane River, B4, B5
Chibito, B5
Chimoio, B3
Chokwe, B5

Democratic Republic of the Congo, A1

Gaza Province, A4, B4, B5
Gorongosa National Park, B2, B3
Great Rift Valley, C1, C2

Inhambane City, B4, B5
Inhambane Province, B4, B5
Inhaminga, B3

Lago Chuali, B5
Lago de Cahora Bassa, A2, B2
Lagoa Poelela, B5
Lake Bangweulu, A1
Lake Kariba, A2
Lake Malawi, B1, B2
Licungo River, C2, C3
Ligonha River, C2, D2
Limpopo River, A4, B4, B5
Lugenda River, C1, C2
Lurio River, C2, D1, D2

Malawi, B1, B2, C1, C2
Manica City, B3
Manica Province, B2—B4
Mapai, B4
Maputo City, B5
Maputo Elephant Reserve, B5
Maputo Province, B5
Massingir, B4
Messalo River, C1, D1

Mount Binga, B3
Mount Namuli, C2
Mozambique Channel, B3—B5, C3—C5, D1—D5

Namaacha, B5
Nampula City, D2
Nampula Province, C2, D1, D2
Namuno, D1
Niassa Province, B1, C1, C2

Pemba, D1
Planalto de Angonia, B2
Planalto Mocambicano, C1, C2
Pungüe River, B3

Quelimane, C3
Quissanga, D1

Revue River, B3
Rovuma River, C1, D1

Save River, B4
Sofala Province, B2—B4, C3

South Africa, A4, A5, B4, B5
Swaziland, A5, B5

Tanzania, B1, C1, D1
Tete City, B2
Tete Province, A2, B2, B3, C3

Xai-Xai, B5

Zambezi River, A2, B2, B3, C3
Zambezia, C2, C3, D2
Zambia, A1, A2, B1, B2
Zimbabwe, A2—A4, B2—B4

ECONOMIC MOZAMBIQUE

Agriculture

- Cattle
- Subsistence Farming
- Sugar
- Tea Plantations

Natural Resources

- Coal
- Gold
- Hydroelectric Power
- **Fe** Iron Ore
- **Mn** Manganese
- Natural Gas
- Tantalite Titanium

Manufacturing

- Basket Weaving
- Steelworks
- Wood Carving

Services

- Airport
- Port
- Tourism

ABOUT THE ECONOMY

All figures are 2017 estimates unless otherwise noted.

GROSS DOMESTIC PRODUCT (GDP, OFFICIAL EXCHANGE RATE)
$14.964 billion (2019)

GDP PER CAPITA (BASED ON PURCHASING POWER PARITY)
$1,300

GDP GROWTH
3.11 percent (2018)

GDP SECTORS
agriculture: 23.9 percent
industry: 19.3 percent
services: 56.8 percent

LABOR FORCE
12.9 million

LABOR FORCE BY OCCUPATION
agriculture: 74.4 percent
industry: 3.9 percent
services: 21.7 percent (2015)

UNEMPLOYMENT RATE
24.5 percent

POPULATION BELOW POVERTY LINE
46.1 percent (2015)

CURRENCY
1 metical (MZN) = 100 centavos
$1 USD = 73.32 meticais (November 2020)

AGRICULTURAL PRODUCTS
cotton, cashew nuts, sugarcane, tea, cassava (manioc, tapioca), corn, coconuts, sisal, citrus and tropical fruits, potatoes, sunflowers; beef, poultry

NATURAL RESOURCES
coal, titanium, natural gas, hydropower, tantalum, graphite

INDUSTRIES
aluminum, petroleum products, chemicals (fertilizer, soap, paints), textiles, cement, glass, asbestos, tobacco, food, beverages

MAJOR EXPORTS
aluminum, prawns, cashews, cotton, sugar, citrus, timber, bulk electricity

MAJOR IMPORTS
machinery and equipment, vehicles, fuel, chemicals, metal products, foodstuffs, textiles

MAJOR TRADING PARTNERS
South Africa, India, Netherlands, China, United Arab Emirates, Portugal

CULTURAL MOZAMBIQUE

Mercado Central Market
This outstanding open-air market sells crafts, food, and household items.

1910 Railroad Station
This railway station features a dome designed by Gustave Eiffel.

Ponta do Ouro
A favorite tourist destination for visitors from South Africa, Ponta do Ouro is known for its excellent beaches and is the prime area for fishing.

Mozambique Isl
This island's his architecture inc the oldest Europea in sub-Saharan Af

Bazaruto Archipelago
Made a national park 1971, the archipelago a great destination bird-watching, snorkeling, sighting whales or dolphi

Inhambane Province Co
This long coast is the coun most highly developed are tourism, with its outstand beaches and wide array water sports.

Maputo's "old town"
This part of the capital is home to historic architecture, including the Iron House.

Inhambane
Here stand many color era buildings, including 18th-century cathedral

ABOUT THE CULTURE

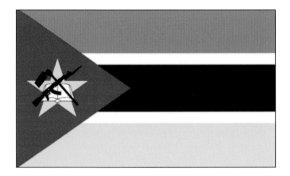

All figures are 2020 estimates unless otherwise noted.

OFFICIAL NAME
Republic of Mozambique

CAPITAL
Maputo

OTHER MAJOR CITIES
Beira, Nampula, Chimoio, Xai-Xai, Inhambane, Quelimane, Angoche, Lumbo

POPULATION
30,098,200

ETHNIC GROUPS
African 99 percent (Makhuwa, Tsonga, Lomwe, Sena, and others), mestiço 0.8 percent, other (includes European, Indian, Pakistani, Chinese) 0.2 percent (2017)

RELIGIOUS GROUPS
Roman Catholic 26.2 percent, Muslim 18.3 percent, Zionist Christian 15.1 percent, Evangelical/Pentecostal 14.7 percent, Anglican 1.6 percent, other 4.7 percent, none 13.4 percent, unspecified 2.5 percent (2019)

LANGUAGES
Makhuwa 26.1 percent, Portuguese (official) 16.6 percent, Tsonga 8.6 percent, Nyanja 8.1 percent, Sena 7.1 percent, Lomwe 7.1 percent, Chuwabo 4.7 percent, Ndau 3.8 percent, Tswa 3.8 percent, other Mozambican languages 11.8 percent, other 0.5 percent, unspecified 1.8 percent (2017)

LIFE EXPECTANCY AT BIRTH
total population: 55.9 years
male: 54.4 years
female: 57.4 years

LITERACY RATE
total population: 60.7 percent
male: 72.6 percent
female: 50.3 percent (2017)

TIMELINE

IN MOZAMBIQUE	IN THE WORLD
1498 Portuguese navigator Vasco da Gama stops at Mozambique Island en route to India.	
1507 Portuguese conquer Mozambique Island; it becomes the capital of Portuguese East Africa.	**1530** The transatlantic slave trade begins.
	1558–1603 Elizabeth I rules England.
early 1600s The Dutch fail in their efforts to capture Mozambique Island.	**1620** Pilgrims sail the *Mayflower* to America.
1600s–1800s Portuguese establish *prazeros* to control the people of the river valleys.	**1776** The U.S. Declaration of Independence is written.
	1789–1799 The French Revolution takes place.
	1861 The American Civil War begins.
1895 The colonial period starts.	**1869** The Suez Canal opens.
1898 Lourenço Marques (later Maputo) becomes the capital.	
1917 The Portuguese put down Makonde rebellion in Zambezia Province, the last tribal uprising against Portugal.	**1914** World War I begins.
1950s Independence movements in Africa begin.	**1939–1945** World War II devastates Europe.
	1945 The North Atlantic Treaty Organization (NATO) is formed.
1962 Front for the Liberation of Mozambique (FRELIMO) is formed.	**1957** The Russians launch *Sputnik 1*.
1964–1975 FRELIMO wages revolution against Portuguese troops.	
1969 Eduardo Mondlane is assassinated.	**1966–1969** The Chinese Cultural Revolution occurs.
1974 Mozambique is granted independence.	

IN MOZAMBIQUE	IN THE WORLD
1975	
FRELIMO gains control of the government; Samora Machel is president.	
1977	
Civil war pits FRELIMO against the forces of RENAMO (Mozambican National Resistance).	**1981**
	The worldwide AIDS epidemic begins.
1986	**1986**
President Samora Machel is killed in a plane crash; Joaquim Chissano becomes president.	A nuclear power disaster occurs at Chernobyl in Ukraine.
1990	
The FRELIMO government's new constitution ends Communism.	**1991**
	The breakup of the Soviet Union occurs.
1992	
Cease-fire treaty ends the civil war.	
1994	
Joaquim Chissano is elected president.	**1997**
1999	Britain returns Hong Kong to China.
Joaquim Chissano is reelected for a five-year term.	**2001**
	Terrorists attack the United States on September 11.
	2008
	Americans elect their first African American president, Barack Obama.
	2009
2011	An outbreak of H1N1 flu spreads around the world.
Gas is discovered off the Mozambican coast.	
2014	
Filipe Nyusi wins presidential election.	**2015–2016**
	ISIS launches terror attacks in Belgium and France.
2017	**2017**
President Nyusi and the RENAMO leader finally end their conflict. Jihadist insurgency begins in Cabo Delgado Province.	Donald Trump becomes U.S. president. Hurricanes devastate Texas, Caribbean islands, and Puerto Rico.
2019	**2019**
Cyclone Idai causes extensive flooding and loss of life in Sofala Province.	Notre Dame Cathedral in Paris is damaged by fire.
2020	**2020**
President Nyusi is inaugurated after winning re-election for final five-year term.	COVID-19 pandemic spreads across the world. Joe Biden wins U.S. presidential election.

GLOSSARY

animism
The attribution of a soul, or spirit, to plants, inanimate objects, and natural phenomena; an aspect of traditional African religions.

assimilados
Under colonialism, Africans who had reached a level of "civilization" according to Portuguese standards.

curandeiros
Faith healers in traditional religions.

FRELIMO
The Mozambican Liberation Front, the center/left-wing, Democratic socialist, ruling political party.

indígenas
In Portuguese, indigenous Africans.

lingua franca
A language that is adopted as a common language between speakers whose native languages are different.

marrabenta
A lively style of Mozambican music.

Marxism-Leninism
The political and economic Communist ideology that formed the guiding doctrine of the Soviet Union and other Communist nations in the 20th century.

matapa
A dish of stewed greens, usually cassava leaves.

mbila (plural *timbila*)
A musical instrument similar to a xylophone, often played by the Chopi people.

mestiço
In Mozambique, a person of mixed Bantu and Portuguese heritage.

não indígenas
Nonindigenous members of colonial Mozambican society—Europeans, Asians, mestiços, and *assimilados*.

paõ
Soft white rolls of Portuguese bread.

piri-piri
A spicy red condiment served with many Mozambican foods.

prazos
Estates in the Zambezi Valley granted by the king of Portugal to European settlers and traders in the 17th to 20th centuries.

RENAMO
The Mozambican National Resistance, a ring-wing, anti-Communist, populist opposition party.

shibalo
A forced labor system introduced by the Portuguese in the early 20th century.

xima (ncima)
A bland, white, pasty dish made from corn flour that forms the foundation of the Mozambican diet.

FOR FURTHER INFORMATION

BOOKS

Briggs, Philip. *Mozambique*. Chalfont St. Peter, UK: Bradt Travel Guides, 2017.

Hansen, Hawa, and Julia Turshen. *In Bibi's Kitchen: The Recipes and Stories of Grandmothers from the Eight African Countries that Touch the Indian Ocean*. Berkeley, CA: Ten Speed Press, 2020.

Lonely Planet. *Zambia, Mozambique, Malawi*. Franklin, TN: Lonely Planet, 2017.

ONLINE

Al Jazeera. "Mozambique Archive." www.aljazeera.com/where/mozambique.

AllAfrica. "Mozambique." allafrica.com/mozambique.

BBC News. "Mozambique Country Profile." www.bbc.com/news/world-africa-13890416.

Britannica. "Mozambique." www.britannica.com/place/Mozambique.

CIA. *The World Factbook*. "Mozambique." cia.gov/library/publications/the-world-factbook/geos/mz.html.

Club of Mozambique. clubofmozambique.com.

Human Rights Watch. "Mozambique." www.hrw.org/africa/mozambique#.

MUSIC

Chopi Music from Mozambique. MW Records, 2009.

Marrabenta Music from Mozambique: Yinguica. Arc Music, 2009.

Sounds of Africa, Yinguica. Arc Music, 2019.

FILMS

Dicing with Death, Episode 4: "Mozambique: Where Life Is the Strongest Thing There Is." Tony Comiti Productions, September 10, 2018.

Green Paradise, Episode 7: "Mozambique: An African Dawn." What's Up Films, Pierre Carrique, 2011.

The Train of Salt and Sugar. Ebano Multimedia, 2016.

BIBLIOGRAPHY

BBC News. "Mozambique Country Profile." www.bbc.com/news/world-africa-13890416.

BBC News. "Mozambique Profile—Timeline." https://www.bbc.com/news/world-africa-13890720.

Chinaka, Cris, Lesley Wroughton, and Joby Warrick. "An Islamist Insurgency in Mozambique Is Gaining Ground—and Showing a Strong Allegiance to the Islamic State." *Washington Post*, November 13, 2020. www.washingtonpost.com/world/africa/mozambique-insurgents-islamic-state/2020/11/13/82d3bc8a-2460-11eb-9c4a-0dc6242c4814_story.html.

CIA. *The World Factbook*. "Mozambique." cia.gov/library/publications/the-world-factbook/geos/mz.html.

Economist Intelligence Unit, The. "Democracy Index 2019." *The Economist Intelligence Unit Limited*, 2020. www.eiu.com/Handlers/WhitepaperHandler.ashx?fi=Democracy-Index-2019.pdf&mode=wp&campaignid=democracyindex2019.

FAO. "Country profile—Mozambique." Food and Agriculture Organization of the United Nations, 2016. www.fao.org/3/i9805en/I9805EN.pdf.

Freedom House. "Freedom in the World 2020: Mozambique." freedomhouse.org/country/mozambique/freedom-world/2020.

Global Hunger Index. "Mozambique." www.globalhungerindex.org/mozambique.html.

Human Rights Watch. "World Report 2020: Mozambique." www.hrw.org/world-report/2020/country-chapters/mozambique#.

Kajjo, Sirwan. "3 Years into Insurgency, Mozambique's Cabo Delgado Remains Vulnerable." *VOA News*, October 7, 2020. www.voanews.com/extremism-watch/3-years-insurgency-mozambiques-cabo-delgado-remains-vulnerable.

Ramsar. "Mozambique." www.ramsar.org/wetland/mozambique.

UNDP Human Development Report 2019. "Mozambique." hdr.undp.org/sites/all/themes/hdr_theme/country-notes/MOZ.pdf.

UNESCO. Intangible Cultural Heritage. "Mozambique." ich.unesco.org/en/state/mozambique-MZ.

UNESCO. World Heritage. "Mozambique." whc.unesco.org/en/statesparties/mz.

US Embassy in Mozambique. "COVID-19 Information." December 3, 2020. mz.usembassy.gov/covid-19-information.

VOA. "Mozambique President, Opposition Leader Sign Peace Agreement." *VOA News*, August 1, 2019. www.voanews.com/africa/mozambique-president-opposition-leader-sign-peace-agreement.

World Food Programme. "Mozambique." www.wfp.org/countries/mozambique.

World Meteorological Organization. "State of the Climate in Africa, 2019." reliefweb.int/sites/reliefweb.int/files/resources/1253_en.pdf.

INDEX

INDEX